RELIGION AND THE STATE

The Making and Testing of an American Tradition

BY
EVARTS B. GREENE

GREAT SEAL BOOKS

A Division of Cornell University Press
ITHACA, NEW YORK

Table of Contents

I

Old World Traditions

THE history of church and state relations is a subject on which many treatises have been written by eminent scholars; these books have, however, been little read except by specialists, chiefly, perhaps, by students of the European Middle Ages. To most Americans of, let us say, forty years ago, the subject seemed to have little relation to current problems. Persons of moderate education could indeed recall more or less vaguely what they had read about such dramatic conflicts between spiritual and temporal authorities as those between the German Emperor Henry IV and Pope Gregory VII, and between Henry II of England and Archbishop Thomas of Canterbury. In the history of modern Europe, the textbooks had something to say about the Religious Wars of the sixteenth and seventeenth centuries; about the rule of *cujus regio, ejus religio* by which German princes were allowed to determine the publicly professed religion of their subjects; and about such comparatively recent happenings as the conflict between Revolutionary France and the Catholic Church, and the Roman question in nineteenth-century Italy.

As for our own American experience, intelligent schoolboys knew something of the Puritan church-state in Massachusetts, as well as the experiments in religious liberty by Lord Baltimore in Maryland, Roger Williams and his associates in Rhode Island, and William Penn in Pennsylvania. Such topics seemed to have their appropriate places in textbooks, although the issues involved were thought to be almost, if not quite, obsolete. They might still trouble Europeans, but we in this enlightened, free, and right-minded republic were thought to have happily settled all that business. Did not our constitutions, state and federal, guarantee to all citizens "the free enjoyment of religious profession and worship without discrimination" and ensure the complete separation of the church from the state—of religion from politics? In our American "contribution to civilization," we had set an example which less fortunate peoples might well follow. In this cheerful assurance we were supported by such distinguished foreign observers as Alexis de Tocqueville and James Bryce. Tocqueville in particular saw in the success of the American experiment a clue to the great European problem of his day—how to reconcile the advance of democracy with the maintenance of the Christian tradition. In his own country these two interests seemed to be in conflict: *"Les hommes religieux combattent la liberté, et les hommes de la liberté attaquent les religions."* In America, on the contrary, he found no church that was hostile to democratic and republican institutions.[1]

Now, however, in these middle years of the twentieth century, we begin to suspect that certain age-old problems are not so simple as they once seemed. In present-day Europe, the church-state issue is one of intensely practical politics, whether in Communist Russia, Fascist Italy, or Nazi Germany. It has also come home to us here through the natural sympathy of religious groups in this country with the victims of totalitarian policies. These old-world conflicts have grown in part out of situations quite different from our own; but some of the factors involved affect us also. Here, too, *laissez-faire* liberalism has—for better or worse— been weakened, governmental functions have expanded, and nationalism is little less intense than it is across the water. As our government extends its control over the economic activities of its citizens, are we sure that

[1] *Démocratie en Amérique* (ed. Paris, 1864), I, 18.

2

this increasingly powerful modern state may not enlarge its control over other social concerns? How far, for instance, may the state go in molding the ideas of youth, without coming into conflict with other corporate loyalties, including those of the churches? Specific examples of the emergence of such issues in this country will be discussed in later lectures; it will be enough here to take a few illustrations from our recent history.

Legislative bodies have enacted or considered measures relating to divorce, birth control, child labor, and the treatment of evolution in the schools. On all these subjects, however, influential religious groups have expressed strong convictions and brought them to bear on legislators. In the presidential election of 1928, one of the major candidates engaged in a serious debate with a prominent citizen of New York on the question whether obedience to the claims of his church was compatible with the free exercise of duties imposed on the President of the United States by his oath of office. In the last Constitutional Convention of the State of New York, the church and state issue was raised in connection with proposed amendments relating to education. Of peculiar interest, because it had the distinction of being cited with approval in a papal encyclical on education, is the decision of the United States Supreme Court in 1925, declaring invalid an Oregon law directed against private and parochial schools. Still more recently, representatives of certain religious denominations have seen in President Roosevelt's appointment of Mr. Myron Taylor to confer with Pope Pius XII on current international problems a menace to our American tradition of separation between church and state.

In short, even in this country questions of church and state are by no means of purely antiquarian interest. In one form or another they are involved in current political and social issues on which our legislators and our voters disagree;

in spite of the efforts of politicians, such questions cannot always be evaded. It seems worth while, therefore, to reconsider the background of our present theory and practice, not only in our colonial and national experience, but in those older societies from which our fathers came, whose usages and mental attitudes largely determined what they thought and did in their new homes across the sea.

The Europe which our pioneer colonists knew had largely broken with the medieval tradition of an international or supernational, Christian commonwealth, whose aspirations were embodied in the Holy Roman Empire and in the Church of Western Christendom with the Roman pontiff at its head; yet in the thinking not only of Catholics but of most Protestants much of that older tradition survived, and students of our early American institutions cannot leave it wholly out of account. In attempting a brief summary of this medieval inheritance, an American who has been occupied chiefly with the history of his own country must tread cautiously if he is to escape the numerous pitfalls besetting the unwary layman. Yet the effort must be made, and on the broad outlines of the picture the experts seem fairly well agreed.

We begin then with the concept of a Christian society, in which spiritual and temporal authorities, both divinely commissioned, were to coöperate in realizing here on earth the City of God. It was the primary business of civil rulers to maintain public order and promote the welfare of their subjects in this present world; in this temporal sphere, it was the duty of every Christian to yield willing obedience. In the frequently quoted words of the Epistle to the Romans: "For there is no power but of God: the powers that be are ordained of God. Whosoever therefore resisteth the power, resisteth the ordinance of God" (Romans XIII, 1, 2). On the other hand, the church, acting through its priesthood, its bishops, and its visible head in Peter's successor, the Bishop of Rome, was concerned with the spiritual and eternal welfare of man. In this higher sphere, the church was entitled to the unquestioning allegiance of all Christians from the humblest serf to the most exalted temporal rulers—magistrates, princes, kings, and the emperor himself. Clergy and laity agreed on this general principle of the two spheres. The good citizen and the good Christian must, in the words of the Gospel text: "Render therefore unto Caesar the things which are Caesar's; and unto God the things that are God's." On the precise application of this principle, however, agreement was not easy then and it is not easy now.

In return for its teaching of obedience to civil rulers, the church as the ultimate authority in matters of faith and morals was entitled to the support of the state in enforcing its decisions. Heresy, once-defined by the church, was subject to civil as well as ecclesiastical penalties—a principle frequently acknowledged in public law from the sixth-century code of Justinian to the fifteenth-century English statute *De haeretico comburendo,* under which heretics duly convicted by a spiritual court were turned over to the secular power for burning at the stake. Heresy was an infection, more deadly than physical disease, from which rulers were bound to protect their people.

Since church and state claimed, in any particular country, the allegiance of the same people, there was naturally much interlocking. The administrative service of the Crown was largely entrusted to ecclesiastics, and the higher clergy were represented in Parliaments. On the other hand, kings and other temporal rulers constantly interfered in the choice of bishops. Many functions now assumed by the state were then dealt with by the church, which was, in a very real sense, a government with a numerous civil service of its own. Under its own canon law, administered through ecclesiastical courts, the church exercised jurisdiction in matrimonial and probate

5

cases, and in criminal cases involving members of the clerical order.

For our present purpose, it is hardly necessary to deal with the mass of controversial material in which the opposing claims of church and state, in the twilight zone between them, were set forth by advocates of one or the other party. Two general notions, however, seem especially important for a twentieth-century American trying, so far as he may, to understand the fundamental differences between medieval modes of thought on this subject and those which seem normal to him. In the first place, most of our fellow citizens think of the acceptance of any religious faith, or membership in any church, as a matter of individual rather than community concern. In medieval society, on the contrary, acceptance of the Christian tradition as authoritatively interpreted by the Catholic Church was, generally speaking, taken for granted; the maintenance of that tradition—its defense against subversive tendencies—was distinctly a community concern, in which the state shared responsibility with the church.

We need, secondly, if we are to orient ourselves in a world so different from our own, to remember that among various claimants to the allegiance of the individual the political state had no such unique and dominating position in medieval society as it has in our modern life. From that earlier point of view, it was limited by divine and natural law; if temporal rulers overstepped those limits, they were confronted not only by individuals or temporary combinations of objectors but by other corporate entities, of which the church was the most pervasive and formidable. Individuals often suffered from the tyranny of one or another of these various authorities; but the assertion from time to time of conflicting claims helped to keep alive the idea of constitutional limitations and in some measure protected liberty against absolutist, or what we now call totalitarian, conceptions of the state. With all its insistence on the duty of the subject to obey the constituted authorities, the church also remembered, in cases of conflict between temporal authority and the divine law, the Scriptural injunction, "We ought to obey God rather than men."

If what has been said so far may be taken as indicating in rough outline essential features of medieval theory and practice, we may ask next how much of this "ideology" survived the Protestant Revolution. Certainly faith in the ideal of a visible Christian commonwealth, international in its scope, had been rudely disturbed. The Holy Roman Empire, as the political embodiment of that commonwealth, had lost whatever authority it had ever possessed as an international institution. The church was indeed still vigorous, having reformed its lines after early reverses and reclaimed much of its lost constituency; still its claim to catholicity was effectively disputed over a great part of Western Christendom. Nevertheless, the conception of religion as a community concern remained in the thought of most of the Protestant Reformers.[2] However much they might assert the right of private judgment, based on independent reading of the Scriptures, most of them looked to their governments for support—in kingdom, principality, or city-state—to defend orthodoxy, as they understood it, against heresy, blasphemy, and "idolatry," by which they commonly meant the worship of the Catholic Church. Thus in Germany, the constituent governments of the Empire, as well as individuals under their authority, were Catholic, Lutheran, or Reformed, according to the determination of their respective sovereigns; subjects were expected to conform to the official system. So it was also with Catholic and Reformed cantons in Switzerland. In the Scan-

[2] Cf. the statement of a recent Catholic writer: "It must be remembered that the conception of the State was then inseparable from that of the Christian religion. If the Protestants abandoned Rome, it was to create a State adhering still more closely, to their mind, to Christian life and faith." L. Sturzo, *Church and State* (London, 1939), 242.

7

dinavian countries, the Lutheran Church was established; even in the comparatively liberal United Provinces of the Netherlands the Reformed faith was specially recognized and supported by measures against Lutherans, as well as Catholics. When the Pilgrims took refuge in Holland, the conflict between strict Calvinists and Arminians within the Reformed Church was an important issue in Dutch politics, and many of the latter were banished by the dominant orthodox party. Though at the close of the sixteenth century, France, after its series of religious wars, conceded a limited toleration to Protestants by the Edict of Nantes, the law expressly recognized the dominant position of the Catholic Church.

Thus the idea of coöperation between church and state survived the Protestant Revolution and was accepted alike by Catholic and Protestant governments. Uniformity, at least in the outward manifestations of religion, was generally regarded as essential to national unity. Actually, secular and religious considerations were so entangled in the policies of states that it is not always easy to say how far one or the other was the more influential in proceedings against dissenters. If the churches relied on temporal sovereigns for support against hostile forces within and without, it was soon evident that some loss of freedom was involved for the church.

In the partnership of church and state, there was in most Protestant countries a tendency for the latter to become the dominant partner. Even an aggressively Catholic prince, like Philip II of Spain, insisted on a considerable measure of control over the clergy in his dominions. On this point I may quote the statement of a Catholic scholar, the Italian writer, Don Luigi Sturzo, in his recent book on *Church and State.* "Post-Tridentine Catholicism," he writes, "had found itself in a position of conflict not only with the Protestant princes, who based their dominion on the reunion in a single head of the temporal and spiritual powers, but also against the Catholic princes, who invaded the ecclesiastical domain and assumed they could direct church affairs in their States." [3] In England and in the Lutheran states especially, the church seemed at times perilously near becoming a department of the state. Of this danger, Calvin, among the leading Protestant Reformers, was most keenly aware; and, as we shall see, his Church-State of Geneva went far in the opposite direction.

Over against the prevailing theory and practice of the dominant churches, there were dissentient minorities, and among them sectarian groups that, as in the case of most Anabaptists, regarded religion as quite outside the sphere of political governments. Their numbers remained comparatively small in most countries and their ideas were usually regarded as subversive, not only by Catholics but by most Protestants. There were also latitudinarian thinkers, including the so-called Socinians, who minimized the importance of traditional dogmas, regarding many of them as nonessential. Such persons naturally favored toleration of what seemed to them more or less indifferent matters, advocating liberty of conscience and worship for all whose teaching did not disturb the peace and safety of the state. They did not oppose some measure of state control, in the interest of public order, over ecclesiastical organizations as corporate bodies within the state. Finally, we have such groups as the *Politiques* in France, who, whether orthodox or indifferent on theological issues, tried to keep religious differences out of politics, while accepting the preferred status of the Catholic Church. Nevertheless, in the general picture of the European scene as it appeared to the pioneers of Virginia and New England, some form of association between state and church seemed the normal practice; separatist ideas were mainly held by comparatively small and uninfluential minorities.

[3] Sturzo, *Church and State*, 249.

Though our seventeenth-century English colonists were aware of developments on the Continent and influenced by what they saw there, they had most definitely in mind conditions in their own country. At this point, therefore, we must pass from generalizations about Europe as a whole to a closer view of the Anglican establishment and the church-state ideas of its Puritan critics.

In the early years of the seventeenth century, the legal framework of the Anglican Church was set by a series of statutes enacted by the Parliaments of the Tudor period, those of Elizabeth's reign confirming with some modifications the legislation of Henry VIII and Edward VI. Largely determined by political considerations, these statutes are marked by an aggressive nationalism, asserting itself against any form of foreign control. Thus the Elizabethan Act of Supremacy is entitled "An Act restoring to the Crown the ancient Jurisdiction over the State Ecclesiastical and Spiritual, and abolishing all Foreign Power repugnant to the same." In the text of the act there are frequent references to "usurped and foreign power," now to be forever extinguished. For the headship of the Pope in the government of the church was now substituted that of the Crown, though the word "Head" used in Henry's Act of Supremacy disappears in the Elizabethan statute. Elizabeth was content to be recognized as "the only Supreme Governor of this realm . . . as well in all spiritual or ecclesiastical things or causes as temporal." She and her successors were vested, in their dominions, with "all manner of jurisdictions, privileges, and preëminences, in any wise touching or concerning any spiritual or ecclesiastical jurisdiction." [4] Medieval conflicts between the Papacy and the King over episcopal elections were now disposed of by giving the Crown full control of such appointments. Elections by cathedral

[4] Tanner, *Tudor Constitutional Documents*, 130–135. In the case of citations lacking full bibliographical data, see the "Bibliographical Notes."

chapters became, as they still are, purely formal, since the royal *congé d'élire*, or permission to elect, was accompanied by a "letter missive" designating the person to be elected. The two great assemblies of the clergy—the Convocations of Canterbury and York—could meet only with the consent of the Crown, and their legislation required the royal assent. Though the Queen made no claim to expertness in matters of doctrine and recognized the Scriptures as the ultimate standard of faith, she did in the last resort, either independently or in Parliament, determine with the help of the clergy as expert consultants what dogmatic teaching, ritual, or church government was permissible in the national church.

The right, assumed by Parliament, to speak for the national church was justified on the ground that it was the only body which represented both clergy and laity. In the words of Professor Pollard, "The circumstance that the bulk of the English people was represented in Parliament, but not in Convocation, has been the decisive factor in the constitutional conflict between *regnum and sacerdotium*," or in plain English, between state and church.[5] Next in importance to the Act of Supremacy in the ecclesiastical legislation of the Elizabethan Parliaments was the Act of Uniformity. This law, following an earlier statute of King Edward's time with some modifications, authorized the Book of Common Prayer with its doctrinal implications as the only legitimate mode of public worship. There were penalties for nonconforming clergy, for those who induced ministers to depart from the prescribed service, and for all subjects who without legitimate excuse failed to attend such services on Sundays and holy-days.[6] So far as the Church of England is concerned, any changes in the Book of Common Prayer require even now

[5] A. F. Pollard, *Evolution of Parliament* (London and New York, Longmans, Green and Company, Inc., 1920), 198.

[6] Tanner, *Tudor Constitutional Documents*, 135–139.

the approval of Parliament—a body that includes, besides members of the Anglican communion, Catholics, various kinds of Protestant dissenters, Jews and other non-Christian persons. Very recently a Parliament so constituted did actually refuse to approve a revision of the Prayer Book proposed by the representatives of the church.

A rationalization of this relationship between church and state may be found in the eighth book of Hooker's monumental work, *Of the Lawes of Ecclesiasticall Politie*, which was written to defend the new order against its Catholic and Puritan critics. Though we cannot be sure how far this particular part of the *Ecclesiastical Polity*, published many years after Hooker's death, preserves his precise language, it is, on the whole, a fair presentation of early Anglican theory.[7] From this point of view, the same people who composed the political community were also members of the church; "seeing that there is not any man of the Church of England but the same man is also a member of the commonwealth; nor any man a member of the commonwealth, which is not also of the Church of England."[8] Thus the church and the commonwealth were conceived as "personally one Society, which society being termed a commonwealth as it liveth under whatsoever form of secular law and regiment, a Church as it hath the spiritual law of Jesus Christ."[9] On this assumption, which hardly corresponded with actual conditions even in Hooker's time, it seemed reasonable that Parliament, the only body which, with its bishops in the House of Lords, represented both clergy and laity, should act in ecclesiastical as well as temporal matters. So, to quote again, Parliament was "a

[7] Cf. R. A. Houk, ed., *Hooker's Ecclesiastical Polity*, Book VIII (New York, 1931).

[8] R. Hooker, *Works* (ed. Keble, Church, and Paget) (Oxford, 1888). III, 330.

[9] *Ibid.*, 334.

court not so merely temporal as if it might meddle with nothing but only leather and wool." [10] It followed that the civil authorities were bound to care for the "eternal safety" of their people as well as for their "temporal peace"; God had not ordained kings "only to fat up men like hogs, and to see that they have their mast." [11] A part of the responsibility assigned to the state was, as in medieval theory, to support with its coercive power the established order in the church. Men's thoughts were doubtless beyond human control; "to prescribe what men shall think belongeth only to God." Yet, "As opinions are either fit or inconvenient to be expressed, so men's law hath to determine of them. It may for public unity's sake require men's professed assent." [12]

Hooker's reference to "professed assent" for "public unity's sake" suggests an essential feature of Elizabethan policy in relation to the church. It was not primarily concerned with doctrinal issues, except so far as such controversies affected the peace and safety of the realm. Its aim was the establishment of a middle way between Rome and Geneva, an establishment sufficiently comprehensive to provide for moderate men of various shades of opinion. When this order was once established, overt opposition to it became a matter of civil disobedience. Such a program did not, however, appeal to men of strong religious convictions among the Catholics, on the one side, and the Puritans on the other. In the case of the Catholics, this political phase of the situation was emphasized after the bull of Pope Pius V (1570), not only excommunicating Elizabeth but absolving her subjects from their allegiance.[13] This was followed by the increased missionary

[10] *Ibid.*, 409.
[11] *Ibid.*, 363.
[12] *Ibid.*, 401.
[13] Camden's translation in Tanner, *Tudor Constitutional Documents*, 143–146.

efforts of seminary priests and Jesuit fathers and a "marked revival of active Catholicism" which stiffened Catholic resistance to conformity by plots against the Queen in the interest of her Scottish cousin, and finally by serious foreign complications culminating in the war with Spain. This situation resulted in a series of penal statutes (1571–1593) directed against "Jesuits, Seminary Priests, and such other like disobedient Persons," and finally the "Act against Popish Recusants," which imposed severe penalties, including confiscation of property in extreme cases, on Catholics who failed to attend the services of the established church. Jesuits and seminary priests who persisted in their activities were liable to the penalties of high treason, and a considerable number were actually executed.[14] Under Elizabeth's successors this penal legislation was not consistently enforced; yet it remained on the statute books and was applied from time to time according to the fluctuations of public opinion. Meantime, the more aggressive Puritans and Protestant sectarians, who denied the royal supremacy in ecclesiastical affairs, persistently absented themselves from the services of the national church, or attended irregular religious services, were made liable to various penalties, including imprisonment, banishment, and, for especially obstinate offenders, confiscation of their estates.

In brief, then, the English Church had to accept a much closer control by the state than in the medieval system. It did, however, preserve—for better or worse—certain privileges: a monopoly of public worship; the exclusion from public office, by the Act of Supremacy, of those who refused to accept the new order; and the right of its bishops to sit in the House of Lords. One form of interlocking between church and state was less common than in the Middle Ages, namely, the holding of state office by members of the clerical order; but it did not cease altogether. Archbishop Laud, for instance, sat not

[14] Tanner, *Tudor Constitutional Documents*, 150–163.

only in the House of Lords but in the Privy Council, and he was in the inner circle of the King's political advisers. His successor as Bishop of London received, to Laud's great satisfaction, the office of Lord High Treasurer.[15] Perhaps the most significant association of church and state for our seventeenth-century colonists was in the government of the English parish, which served both ecclesiastical and secular purposes. The local parson, who has been called "the principal parochial personage," was ordained by his bishop; but he was commonly the nominee of a local magnate who owned the "living." He was charged with the "cure of souls"; but he had also more mundane functions assigned him by act of Parliament, including attendance on the public whipping of "sturdy" rogues and signing the required certificate returning each offender to his home. His church wardens and vestry were, in addition to their responsibility for enforcing church attendance and caring for the church property, also agents of the central government for the administration of such matters as poor relief, the game laws, the control of vagrancy, the regulation of weights and measures, and the punishment of drunkenness. Quite in accord with Hooker's theory of identity of membership in church and commonwealth, all inhabitants of the community were bound not only to attend church, but to pay the parish rate levied by the church wardens and vestry.[16]

This, then, was the church-state system familiar to our early colonists. Not less significant for American beginnings was the social philosophy of its Puritan critics, which had its roots in the theory of Calvin's *Institutes of the Christian Religion*, and the exemplification of that theory in the Church-State of Geneva which was dominated by his personality. If, as Professor Morison has said, the Puritans of early New England had less to say of Calvin than of certain

[15] Article on William Juxon in *Dictionary of National Biography*.
[16] Tanner, *Tudor Constitutional Documents*, 508–510.

15

English exponents of Calvinism,[17] that is comparable with the fact that Newtonian philosophy became implicit in the thinking of many persons who never read Newton's *Principia*. It is, for instance, a significant fact, noted by the late Professor Foster, that fourteen English translations of Calvin's catechism were printed before the Puritan exodus to New England.[18]

When Calvin wrote the section on Church and State in his *Institutes*, he was impressed by the danger to Protestantism from two opposite directions. On one side were the radicals who discredited the Reformation by associating it with theories tending to subvert the social order. These were "the frantic and barbarous men," who would "overturn the order established by God." On the other hand, he feared the consequence of conceding too much power to temporal rulers; there were unfortunately those who flattered princes, "extolling their power without measure," and not hesitating "to oppose it to the government of God." As against the radicals who threatened public order, he insisted on the divine authority of the state. For him as for the early Christian Church, obedience was due even to unworthy rulers; if they were unjust or impious, their punishment must be left to God.[19] Throughout his career, this principle of nonresistance was an essential part of Calvin's teaching. As he wrote to Coligny, the French Huguenot leader, it was better that the "children of God" should perish than "that the Gospel should be dishonored by bloodshed." [20] Nevertheless, we cannot ignore

[17] Samuel Eliot Morison, *The Puritan Pronaos* (New York, 1936), 10.

[18] H. D. Foster, *Collected Essays* (privately printed, 1929), p. 52, note 2. This article on "Calvin's Programme for a Puritan State" is also in *Harvard Theological Review*, October 1908.

[19] Calvin, *Institutes of the Christian Religion* (ed. H. Beveridge), Book IV, chap. XX, §§ 1, 2, 5.

[20] Allen, *Political Thought in the Sixteenth Century*, 53–59, citing Bonnet, *Lettres Françaises*, II, 382.

two other passages that indicate certain limitations of this general principle. One of them goes back to the frequently quoted Scripture text: "We must obey God rather than men." "We are," said Calvin, "subject to the men who rule over us, but subject only in the Lord. If they command anything against him, let us not pay the least regard to it. . . ." Though Calvin probably had in mind here only passive resistance—refusal to obey rather than the use of force—it is hardly surprising that many of his followers should have failed to make this distinction. A second qualification of the general principle of obedience to the Sovereign applied to political systems, in which constitutional checks upon princes were entrusted to certain magistrates or representative bodies. It was not only the right but the duty of such agencies "to check the undue license of Kings." [21]

If all deference was due to the civil authorities in temporal matters, it was essential that the church should be free in spiritual concerns. Calvin would not "allow men at pleasure to enact laws concerning religion and the worship of God." Here, as in the medieval church, the primary responsibility and the right of decision rested with the church; the duty of the state was to accept that decision and see that it was enforced; in the language of the *Institutes*, it was "to foster and maintain the external worship of God, to defend sound doctrine, and the condition of the Church." In particular, the "civil order" must "prevent the true religion, which is contained in the law of God, from being with impunity openly violated and polluted by public blasphemy." [22]

For the working out of these theories, Calvin had an excellent laboratory, so to speak, in the City-State of Geneva, which had lately been emancipated from its former ecclesi-

[21] *Institutes*, Book IV, chap. XX, §§ 30–32. He refers also (§ 30) to "avengers" raised up by God "to punish accursed tyranny."
[22] *Ibid.*, §§ 2, 3.

astical and civil authorities. Here, in sharp contrast with the Tudor system in England, the church was distinctly the stronger partner, and civil rulers as well as ordinary citizens were subject to ecclesiastical discipline. The church was governed by two councils: one composed of the clergy; the other, called the consistory, included the clergy with lay elders, who were named by the civil authorities but virtually chosen by Calvin and his associates. The consistory became a court for the trial of a great variety of offenses against morals and, with the coöperation of the municipal authorities, administered a drastic discipline upon all citizens. Persons excommunicated by the church were debarred from public office and, if not submissive, might be banished from the city. The church defined heresy and determined the guilt of particular persons; but in serious cases ecclesiastical discipline was enforced by the civil government. The outstanding instance of such action by the state on the initiative of the church is, of course, that of Servetus, who was burned at the stake for his attack on the doctrine of the Trinity. In brief, then, the association of church and state was quite as close in Geneva as in the Tudor system, but with this important difference, that the Calvinist clergy had, so to speak, the whip hand.[23]

Calvin died in 1564, five years after the passage of the English Acts of Supremacy and Uniformity, embodying theories and practices of which the Puritans heartily disapproved. For three quarters of a century, they were mainly confined to the role of critics, and to proposals which they could not carry into effect. The controversial literature of the period, however, shows that most of them were fundamentally in accord with Calvin. Like him they found in the Bible not only a definite body of doctrine, but authoritative guid-

[23] See H. D. Foster, "Calvin's Programme for a Puritan State in Geneva, 1536–1541," in *Harvard Theological Review*, I, 391–434; or in his *Collected Essays*, pp. 30 ff.

ance in matters of worship and ecclesiastical discipline. Their ideal church must be free from interference in spiritual concerns; but, like most of their contemporaries, both Catholic and Protestant, they believed that their decisions in that field should be accepted by the state and receive its active support. This was the position taken by Thomas Cartwright and Walter Travers, two of the outstanding Puritan leaders of the sixteenth century, both recognized as such by Hooker in the *Ecclesiastical Polity*. According to Travers, civil rulers were bound to "renounce in themselves and to abolish from amongst their people, all false worship and idolatrie . . . and to establish in all partes the trew worship of God"—all this, of course, as determined by the church in accordance with what was believed to be the clear teaching of the Scriptures.[24] In short, what the early Puritans wished was the reformation of the Church of England, directed by men like themselves. They had no objection to a national church so reformed, and had no idea of dispensing with the coercive power of the state.

As Professor Jordan has pointed out in his excellent study of this subject, most of the Puritans of the early seventeenth century occupied nearly the same position as their Elizabethan predecessors. They too expected, if they gained control, the coöperation of the magistrate "in the creation of a Church that would advance the Kingdom of God on Earth." In particular, he should aid this reformed church by using "the temporal sword for the rooting out of heresy and blasphemy."[25] Even the Congregationalists, on the left wing of the Puritan movement, who regarded the church as a voluntary association of believers, were not always consistent in renouncing the coöperation of the state for the maintenance of true religion and the repression of heresy. Thus John Robin-

[24] *Defence of Ecclesiastical Discipline*, quoted in W. K. Jordan, *Development of Religious Toleration in England*, I, 246.

[25] Jordan, *Development of Religious Toleration in England*, II, 206 ff.

son, the pastor of the Pilgrim Church at Leyden, held in opposition to the Baptists that, though a civil ruler might not determine religious matter "otherwise than Christ hath appoynted," Scripture teaching did not exclude the use of civil power "lawfully for the furtherance of Christ's Kingdom and Lawes." [26]

With due allowance for a number of small groups, which not only withdrew from the Church of England but advocated the complete separation of the church from the state, we may fairly take, as representing the great majority of Puritans, the policy of that party in the House of Commons. In 1629, just before Parliament was dissolved by King Charles and in the same year in which John Winthrop and his associates signed the famous Cambridge Agreement out of which developed a new Puritan commonwealth across the sea, the House adopted a formal "Protestation" against the policies of the Crown. The first paragraph of that document deals with religion and illustrates the close association of religion with politics in the minds of its supporters. When this protest was adopted, Puritan feeling against Archbishop Laud and his followers had been intensified by the so-called Arminian movement, which seemed to be moving the Church of England still further away from the Protestant, or Calvinist, position. Associated with this doctrinal tendency in the minds of the Puritans were the restoration of pre-Reformation forms of service and Laud's drastic treatment of the Puritan clergy. We need to keep this background in mind in order to understand the language of the "Protestation": "Whoever shall bring in innovation of religion, or by favour or countenance seem to extend or introduce Popery or Arminianism, or other opinion disagreeing from the true and orthodox church, shall be reputed a capital enemy to this Kingdom and Commonwealth." [27] In short, Laud and his

[26] *Ibid.*, 242 ff.
[27] Gardiner, *Constitutional Documents of the Puritan Revolution*, 16.

Puritan opponents, though disagreeing as to what was orthodox in doctrine and modes of worship, were equally sure that orthodoxy, as one or the other understood it, was entitled to the support of the state.

In the discussion of church and state relations during the post-Reformation period, much more might well have been said about current theories of toleration. In the various communions, Catholic and Protestant, Anglican and Puritan, toleration in some form and liberty of conscience had their advocates. Sometimes, as in the case of the French *Politiques,* practical considerations prevailed; others, however, were genuinely concerned with the inherent right of the individual to believe and to worship according to the dictates of his own conscience. Many who favored, or accepted, some form of association or coöperation between church and state were nevertheless willing in varying degrees, to tolerate differences in faith and worship. Others went further and favored complete separation—noninterference by the state for or against any particular faith. For such persons, adhesion to any church meant simply voluntary association with other like-minded individuals. To this latter group we shall return when we come to the story of colonial dissent. For the present, we must content ourselves with summarizing very briefly the results of our survey up to this point.

It is clear that the prevailing opinion in Western Christendom generally, and specifically in the England from which our early colonists came, accepted the general idea of a Christian society for whose maintenance and protection against subversive influences the state, as well as the church, was responsible. What form such coöperation should take was a question about which men differed. On the one side, we have the Tudor establishment, which held to the close association of ecclesiastical and temporal authority in the royal supremacy, and whose policies were largely influenced by political considerations.

Even sovereigns who acknowledged their allegiance to the Papacy, went far in their effort to control ecclesiastical affairs within their own dominions. On the other hand, we have, both among Catholics and in the Genevan system of Calvin, a marked reaction against extreme forms of state control, with more emphasis on the independence of the church in its own spiritual sphere. Notwithstanding these—by no means unimportant—differences, all the major religious groups desired and, when in power, secured the more or less active support of the state.

II

European Ideas Transplanted

HAVING examined the theory and practice of church and state relations in the Europe from which our earliest colonists migrated to Virginia and New England, we have now to consider how much of this old-world heritage was transferred to the new commonwealths across the sea. Before, however, taking up the pioneer English colonies with which we are primarily concerned, we shall be helped to a better perspective, if we take note of institutional developments in the American dependencies of other European peoples—in New Spain, New France, and New Netherland. Aside from the advantage of comparative views, we should not wholly ignore some points of contact, significant for our present study, among these various communities. Thus in the case of New Netherland, the importance of the Dutch establishment for the ecclesiastical development of New York is obvious. Again, the Quebec Act enacted by the British Parliament partly to conciliate the French Canadian clergy had a significant relation to the propaganda of our own revolutionary movement. Another interesting circumstance is the fact that the first case referred by President Theodore Roosevelt to the newly created Hague Tribunal, the so-called "Pious Fund" dispute between the United States and Mexico, went back to ecclesiastical relations in New Spain. More recently still, Mexican church-state issues have to some extent complicated the problems of American diplomacy.

The Spanish kings in the age of colonization illustrate admirably the combination of thoroughgoing orthodoxy with aggressive insistence on the royal prerogative in the temporal concerns of the church within their own dominions. For various reasons the association of church and state was closer in the Spanish colonies than in Spain itself, and the extent of royal control in ecclesiastical affairs much greater. The crusading and missionary spirit stimulated by the wars against the Moors was an important element in the minds of Columbus and his royal patrons, and served to justify larger concessions by the papacy to royal authority. Again, the remoteness of the colonies naturally interfered with effective direction from Rome of the Indian missions and the colonial churches. It must be remembered that the Congregation *de Propaganda Fide*, now the central missionary organization of the Catholic Church, was not instituted until 1622, and even then developed its control slowly.[1]

In the colonies, as in the mother country, uniformity in religion was considered essential and immigration was strictly controlled in order to secure a religiously homogeneous population. The number of heretical immigrants was therefore comparatively few, and when such persons appeared they were rigorously dealt with, by the Inquisition or otherwise. The state also gave to the service of the church important material resources as well as effective political support. It was mainly on the clergy, secular and regular, that the colonial administration relied for the controlling, civilizing, and Christianizing of the Indians; clerics were sometimes appointed to important posts in the provincial governments. Throughout the colonial period, the church had to pay for whatever favors it received from the Crown by serious limitations on its freedom. Major ecclesiastical appointments were made on presentation by the King or his representatives. By a

[1] W. R. Corrigan, *Die Kongregation de Propaganda Fide und ihre Tätigkeit in Nord-Amerika* (Munich, 1928), chap. II.

decree of Philip II, ecclesiastics who accepted such appointments without having been duly presented by royal authority were punishable by banishment. Members of the clergy, secular or regular, had to have the royal license for going to, or leaving, the colonies, and their movements while there were supervised by the provincial authorities. Royal consent was also required for the establishment of new churches or convents; papal bulls or briefs could not be circulated in the colonies without inspection and approval by the Council of the Indies—an approval frequently withheld. Other forms of state control were the requirement of government approval for the holding of church assemblies or the publication of their decisions, and the right of the civil administration to define the boundaries of dioceses and parishes. There were ecclesiastical courts in the colonies, including the Inquisition; but matters relating to church patronage were dealt with by the secular courts; disputes between secular and ecclesiastical jurisdictions were determined by the viceroy; and the tribunals of the Spanish Inquisition were set up by royal authority.[2]

In short, the association of church and state in Spanish America was of the closest kind, often involving serious interference with the normal exercise of papal authority. In the words of a Spanish writer, "the Kings of Spain came to acquire such a hand in the ecclesiastical government of America, that with the exception of the purely spiritual, they exercised an authority which appeared to be pontifical. . . . Always the civil power interposes itself between our Church and the Supreme Pastor."[3]

When Philip II died in 1598, the pattern of church-state relations for Spanish America had been substantially deter-

---

[2] Mecham, *Church and State in Latin America*, chaps. I ff.

[3] Quoted, *ibid.*, 43. Cf. Corrigan, *Kongregation de Propaganda*, "Es wurde gut für die Kirche gesorgt, aber sie durfte nicht selbstständig handeln" (p. 49).

mined. In New France, the development was later and more gradual, for permanent colonization did not begin until the early seventeenth century. Among the abortive projects of the sixteenth century, during the period of the Religious Wars, some had been promoted by Protestants; and even in Canada, the policy of a definitely Catholic colony was not fixed until, in 1627, the administration was entrusted to the Company of the Hundred Associates. There were Huguenots in the company under whose auspices Champlain founded Quebec, and there were others of that faith among the early traders on the St. Lawrence. It was under the administration of Richelieu, who was responsible for the charter to the Hundred Associates, that the main outlines of church-state policy for New France were determined—to be developed further under Louis XIV, when the government of the colony was taken over by the Crown.

Under the charter of the Associates, the company agreed to settle several thousand native-born French Catholics in the colony; foreigners and Protestants were to be excluded. Although there are references thereafter to heretics in the colony, they were largely temporary employees and never formed more than an insignificant fraction of the population. In New France, as in New Spain, the state recognized only one church, and though conflicts between the two authorities occurred from time to time the relation between them was essentially one of coöperation. One phase of this relation was the active patriotism of the French Jesuits, on whom the colony largely depended for maintaining friendly relations with the Indians. The financial support of the church came largely from the Crown, which made large grants of land to the religious orders, notably to the Jesuits and the Ursuline nuns. Royal contributions of money also supplemented the revenue from tithes for the parochial clergy, and provided an endowment for the bishopric of Quebec. Here, as in New Spain, the Indian missions were regarded as a prime object of governmental, as well as ecclesiastical, concern. Aside from the economic support received from the state, the church was represented in the provincial government through the bishop, who sat with the governor, intendant, and other lay members in the Sovereign Council of the province. When that Council was organized in 1663, the selection of its first members was entrusted to Bishop Laval and the newly arrived governor; in fact, the choice was practically that of the Bishop, who had with his ecclesiastical associates brought about the removal of the governor's predecessor.[4] The relative influence of the bishop, in comparison with that of the governor and the intendant, naturally varied according to their personal characteristics and there were times of acute conflict among these functionaries; but, as already suggested, such conflicts between spiritual and temporal authorities were perhaps a less important phase of Canadian history than has sometimes been supposed.[5]

If the Crown, especially in the days of Louis XIV, was genuinely concerned with the spiritual welfare of his Canadian subjects and their Indian neighbors, the royal prerogative was not forgotten. The Most Christian King, like his Catholic Majesty in Spain, combined doctrinal orthodoxy and the recognition of papal authority in things purely spiritual with a keen desire to be master in his own house. Following an agreement between Louis XIV and Pope Clement X, the right of nomination to the bishopric of Quebec was expressly conceded to the King (1674).[6] Tithes for the support of the

[4] R. Cahall, *Sovereign Council of New France* (New York, 1915), 21–23.

[5] W. B. Munro, *Crusaders of New France* (New Haven, 1918), 127; Eastman, *Church and State in Early Canada*, 263. Eastman says of the siuation at the close of the seventeenth century that "theocratic power was on the wane, with the political balance shifting toward secular men."

[6] Riddell, *Rise of Ecclesiastical Control*, 112, quoting the papal bull of October 1, 1674.

clergy were regulated by the government, which on one occasion reduced the amount to be collected and at other times refused increases proposed by the clergy. As in Spanish America, the founding of new religious establishments required royal approval; letters patent for such institutions might be refused even when authorized by the bishop.[7] The Crown intervened in disputes between the bishop and the religious orders, checked the use of excommunication to enforce the payment of tithes, intervened to prevent removal of parish priests by the bishop, and controlled the reception of papal bulls.[8]

In brief, then, both the great Catholic colonizing powers actively supported the spiritual mission of the church and suppressed dissent; but they also insisted on a very large control of ecclesiastical affairs by the state.

In striking contrast with conditions in New France, where the promotion of Christianity and the securing of an ecclesiastically homogeneous population were major interests of the state, was the situation in New Netherland. There, partly as a matter of conscious policy, and partly through indifference on the part of the mercantile corporation in Holland which governed the colony, there developed a population conspicuous for the variety of its religious elements—Calvinists, Lutherans, Mennonites, Quakers, Catholics, and Jews, all found their way to New Netherland before the English conquest. Yet even here the sense of community concern for religion was not wholly lacking. In one of the earliest pronouncements of the Dutch West India Company—the Charter of Freedoms and Exemptions of 1629—the Patroons and colonists were directed to "find out ways and means whereby they may support a Minister and Schoolmaster, that thus the

[7] *Ibid.*, 116–118, 120 and note.
[8] *Ibid.*, 120–130; with documents cited in the notes.

service of God and zeal for religion may not grow cool and be neglected among them."[9] The Company was not only concerned with religion in general, but with the maintenance of a particular church. "And no other Religion," so reads one article of the new charter of "Freedoms and Exemptions," issued in 1640, "shall be publicly admitted in New Netherland except the Reformed, as it is at present preached and practiced by public authority in the United Netherlands." To this end, the Company was required to provide suitable clergy. In short, the preferred church of the mother country was to be the state church of the colony.[10] In accordance with this policy, the Dutch West India Company regularly supplied Reformed ministers selected by the Classis of Amsterdam, which became the ecclesiastical superior of the colonial churches.

While maintaining an established church, the Company and its official representatives in New Netherland pursued during most of the Dutch period a policy of tolerance toward individuals of differing creeds, distinguishing, however, between liberty of conscience and private devotions, on the one side, and public worship. During the early years of the colony, no group of dissenters was sufficiently numerous to raise the issue of public worship; but the situation gradually changed. The migration of New England Puritans, especially on Long Island, presented in this respect no serious difficulty. They were, after all, Calvinist in doctrine; and the towns which they settled were allowed to form churches in the "New England way." More serious was the question of the Lutherans. Comparatively few in numbers at first, some of them worshiped with the Reformed congregation; but later, reinforced by immigration, they asked permission to hold public services

---

[9] E. B. O'Callaghan, ed., *Documents Relative to the Colonial History of the State of New York* (Albany, 1853), II, 557.

[10] H. Hastings, ed., *Ecclesiastical Records, New York*, I, 130.

with a minister of their own.[11] Unfortunately for them, the strenuous Peter Stuyvesant, then at the head of the government, disapproved. In this course, he was supported by the Calvinist clergy in Holland and in the colony; and the Directors of the Dutch West India Company acquiesced in the order of Stuyvesant and his Council for the expulsion of a Lutheran minister. They urged, however, more conciliatory methods and disapproved the governor's imprisonment of recalcitrant Lutherans. In particular, Stuyvesant was directed not to interfere with religious meetings in private houses.[12]

Stuyvesant, himself an elder in the Dutch Reformed Church, was troubled by other dissenting groups which held irregular meetings in various localities. In 1656, he was responsible for an ordinance imposing heavy fines upon unlicensed preachers and attendants at their meetings, though denying any intention of interfering with freedom of conscience for individuals or with family worship.[13] Among the sectaries who suffered most severely from Stuyvesant's intolerance were the Quakers; and here the authorities in Holland intervened. In 1663, the year before Stuyvesant had to surrender the province to the English, the Company reproved him for banishing a Quaker. It professed no liking for sectaries; but it did not wish to discourage immigration. "You may therefore," wrote the Company, "shut your eyes." It was pointed out that a policy of moderation toward dissenters had worked well in Amsterdam, where it had brought a "considerable influx of people."[14] Increase in population was obviously an important consideration at a time when the independence of the colony was threatened by the English. During the Stuyvesant regime, there was also some anti-Semitic agitation.

[11] *Ibid.*, I, 317 ff., 358–359.
[12] *Ibid.*, I, 352, 423, *et passim.*
[13] *Ibid.*, I, 343.
[14] *Ibid.*, 530.

In 1656, Dominie Megapolensis of New Amsterdam complained that the Jews were increasing in numbers, that more were expected, and that there was talk of building a synagogue. He hoped the Company would send away "these godless rascals"; there were already too many sects. Stuyvesant sympathized with this view, but again the authorities in Holland intervened and revoked an order excluding certain Jewish traders. The Jews were not to hold public office or keep "open retail shops"; but they might "quietly and peaceably carry on business as before, and exercise in all quietness their religion within their houses." [14a]

The ecclesiastical policy of New Netherland was thus far from simple. The Dutch Reformed Church had its preferred status, with the exclusive right of public worship. The administration was also from time to time under pressure from the clergy in Holland and America to take more drastic measures against dissenters, and during Stuyvesant's rule this intolerant element found in him an active ally. On the other hand, the trading interest of the governing corporation in the Netherlands favored toleration, at least for individuals who made no trouble for the government. Consequently, when Stuyvesant's government adopted extreme measures, the Company either interposed its veto or urged moderation. There was no question here of religious equality or the separation of the church from the state; but it is clear that the clergy of New Netherland, like those of the United Provinces, were in no position to realize the theocratic ideals of Calvin.

We turn now to the church-state policies of the English in Virginia and New England, representing, respectively, the Anglican system of the mother country and the Puritan ideals of the English opposition.

The planting of Virginia, by a commercial corporation but under the special patronage of the Crown, was more nearly a

[14a] *Ibid.*, 334–346, 348, 352.

national enterprise than that of any other Continental English colony during this period. The grantees, under the second charter especially, were numerous and fairly representative of the governing classes, including many members of Parliament and several Church of England clergy. This national character was emphasized when the Company government was abolished and Virginia became a royal province, as it continued to be throughout the colonial period, with the exception of a short interval during the Puritan regime in England. It was natural, then, that those who directed the affairs of the colony at home and in America should accept, so far as local conditions permitted, institutional ideas and practices to which they had been accustomed.

Though religion had no such importance in the program of the Virginia promoters as it had in New France, New Spain, or New England, it was not ignored either by the authorities in England or by the early settlers. The royal charter of 1606 emphasized the missionary motive for colonization—to propagate the Christian religion among the natives, who lived in "miserable ignorance of the true knowledge and worship of God." This religious motive was again asserted in the second Virginia charter, and the earliest royal instructions to the Company required the maintenance of religious services for the settlers. There was no doubt either as to what was meant by the "true knowledge and worship of God."[15] It was that of the Church of England, according to the doctrine and rites established by law. To this end, and particularly to exclude persons who affected "the superstitions of the Church of Rome," the charter of 1609 required all emigrants to take the oath of supremacy. The Company recognized its responsibility for sending out ministers of the Church of England and providing for their support. During its administration of the colony, church attendance was required, and in the years of

[15] Brown, *Genesis of the United States*, I, Docs., nos. v, vi, lxvi.

autocratic government before the meeting of the first representative assembly severe penalties were imposed for profanity, blasphemy, and speaking against "the knowne articles of the Christian faith."

With the meeting of the pioneer assembly at Jamestown in 1619, we get a better indication of opinion among the actual settlers. In the first enactments of this body, among those designated as drawn "out of every man's private conceipte," there were several regulations on the subject of religion. Ministers were required to read every Sunday the church service in the Anglican form and there were fines for nonattendance. Provision was soon made by the assembly for the payment of tithes; no man should dispose of his tobacco before the minister's claim was satisfied.[16]

After the revocation of the Company's charter, the royal governors were instructed to see that the Anglican service was regularly observed throughout the province and a competent maintenance provided for the clergy. Among the governor's ecclesiastical functions was that of inducting into office clergymen who had received episcopal ordination in the Church of England. This extension of the Anglican system to the province was not only the clearly defined policy of the Crown; it was also, in the main, supported by colonial opinion. During the seventeenth century, except for a few years during the Puritan regime in England, the Virginia legislation established a system of church and state relations, substantially in accord with the principles of the Tudor-Stuart establishment in England.

Tithes for the parish clergy were required by law and payable by the inhabitants regardless of religious preference. To quote the language of an early statute: "It is thought fitt that all those that work in the ground of what qualitie or condition

[16] L. G. Tyler, ed., *Narratives of Early Virginia* (New York, 1907), 271–273; Hening, *Statutes of Virginia*, I, 122–124.

soever, shall pay tithes to the ministers." [17] In the earlier years the payment required was ten pounds of tobacco and a bushel of corn. At one time when tobacco prices were low, the minister was allowed other payments in kind; but payments in tobacco soon became the standard method. Besides the tithes, every parson was entitled to a piece of land, called the glebe. Parish churches were also built by local taxation. In Virginia as in England, all ministers had to "conforme themselves in all thinges according to the cannons of the Church of England." Laymen were expected to attend church services, and fines for absence, as well as for other irregular conduct on Sundays, were actually enforced. Sabbatarian regulations, though less strenuously applied than in New England, were by no means a dead letter. The established church was also protected by special legislation against dissenters. Puritan clergy were banished for failing to conform to the Anglican services; Quakers were fined, imprisoned, and banished; an early statute not only disqualified Catholics for public office, but provided for the prompt expulsion of any priest who ventured to enter the colony; there were penalties also for persons who, having scruples against infant baptism, failed to present their children for christening.[18]

Though the colonial church received substantial support from the state, it was at a serious disadvantage in other respects. It was in the anomalous situation of an episcopal church, without a bishop nearer than three thousand miles away. Gradually during the first century of colonization, the Bishop of London came to be regarded as the diocesan authority for the colonies; no ministers were to serve Virginia parishes without the Bishop's certificate of orthodoxy. Nevertheless, he could do little either for the discipline of the clergy or the pro-

[17] Act of 1629, Hening, *Statutes*, I, 144.

[18] Bruce, *Institutional History of Virginia*, I, Part I; Hening, *Statutes*, I, *passim*, e.g. 141, 149, 155 ff., 180, 268.

tection of their interests against encroachments by the provincial government or the parish vestries. Near the end of the seventeenth century, the situation was slightly improved by the Bishop's appointment of a resident commissary, who became a member of the provincial council; but this officer could not perform the important episcopal functions of confirmation and clerical ordination. The former rite was allowed to lapse, and candidates for ordination had to cross the ocean. The induction of parish clergy, if and when they were presented by the local vestries, was made the duty of the governor; but the ceremony was often dispensed with by the vestries, which preferred annual contracts with the parson to the more permanent relation resulting from induction.[19] In the absence of effective ecclesiastical discipline, the civil authorities took matters into their own hands and the conduct of the parish clergy was regulated by act of assembly. One such act required every minister "having no lawful impediment" to preach at least one sermon every Sunday, and to give half an hour a week to catechizing the youth and other ignorant persons in his parish, instructing them in the articles of religion. His personal conduct was also regulated by law, and failure of duty on his part was to be duly presented by the churchwardens. In the absence of a regular church court, the General Court, consisting of the governor and council, could deal with the clergy.[20]

In early Virginia, as in England, religious and secular affairs were associated in local administration. Churchwardens and parish vestries, originally elected but commonly filling their own vacancies, chose the ministers and cared for the church property; they also investigated cases of immorality,

[19] Cross, *Anglican Episcopate and the American Colonies*, chaps. I, II; W. S. Perry, *Historical Collections Relating to the American Colonial Church*, I, 261–318.

[20] Hening, *Statutes*, I, 157; III, 289. Cf. Bruce, *Institutional History of Virginia*, I, 69.

which were duly presented by the churchwardens to the county court, administered poor relief, apprenticed orphans, and levied parish taxes for local purposes. In the administration of such duties they were supervised by the justices of the peace.[21]

The pattern thus set for Virginia was subsequently applied with varying success in other royal provinces; but in no other English colony on the Continent was the Anglican system in effective operation before the last decade of the seventeenth century, when, after the temporary overthrow of Lord Baltimore's government, the Church of England was established by law in Maryland. Even in Virginia, liberalizing influences gradually began to make themselves felt; none of the newer provinces had an establishment equal in prestige to that of the "Old Dominion."

In all the provincial establishments so far discussed, the colonial church was dependent, to a greater or less extent, on civil and ecclesiastical authorities in Europe. In New England, on the contrary, during most of the seventeenth century, the dominant Puritan churches could proceed with little or no external control to develop their own institutional life, their modes of worship, and their doctrinal standards, subject only to such limitations as might be involved in their relations with the autonomous commonwealths which they served and on whose sympathetic coöperation they could ordinarily rely. In this freedom from interference, the Puritan leaders of New England had an opportunity comparable with that of Calvin in Geneva. These commonwealths differed, however, from their European counterpart in one important respect. Though their clergy were extremely influential and highly valued as consultants, there was no one overshadowing clerical personality comparable with that of Calvin; in the building of their Christian societies, therefore, the layman's part was much more significant than in Geneva.

[21] Bruce, *ibid.*, I, Part I, chaps. VII–IX.

Of the four Puritan colonies which formed the New England Confederation, Plymouth is comparatively unimportant for our present purpose. Founded by separatists who hoped to lay a "good foundation" for "propagating and advancing the Gospell of the Kingdom of Christ in those remote parts of the world," the Pilgrims represented what might then be called the left wing of English Puritanism. When, however, the founders of Massachusetts Bay adopted the Congregational system of church government, the differences between the two groups faded out. Though the civic leaders of Plymouth were more moderate in action than the leaders of the Bay Colony, they were not consistently separatist in the sense of complete detachment of the church from the state. Though at first contributions for the support of the church were voluntary, the magistrates were after a time authorized to put delinquents "upon their duty." [22] There was no formal church-membership qualification for voters; but in the later years of the colony they had to be certified as "orthodox in the fundamentals of religion." [23] Finally, Plymouth, like most of the other colonies, enacted legislation against Quakers and other heretical persons.[24]

Much the most important colony for the study of Puritan theory and practice is Massachusetts Bay. Its population was much larger than that of all the other New England colonies combined; its leaders had a clearly defined philosophy of church and state relations; and for more than half a century the ruling class worked out its program with remarkable consistency and success. Beginning with what was essentially a commercial charter, they took advantage of a loophole in that document to make it the constitution of an almost completely

[22] W. Walker, *History of the Congregational Churches in the United States* (New York, 1894), 233.

[23] Osgood, *American Colonies in the Seventeenth Century*, I, 298.

[24] *Ibid.*, I, 288.

self-governing state. By the Cambridge Agreement of 1629, the possession of the charter and of the powers conferred by it passed into the hands of a few leaders of whom John Winthrop was, or became, the most influential. The point of view of this English country gentleman and his associates appears in the opening sentence of the Cambridge Agreement, which emphasizes their desire to serve "God's glory and the churches good." [25] It is more definitely explained in a discourse entitled "A Modell of Christian Charity," which Winthrop addressed to his associates on their voyage to New England. In this address, he described himself and his fellow voyagers as a "Company professing ourselves fellow members of Christ," whose purpose it was to establish a community "under a due form of Government both civill and ecclesiasticall." They had entered into a covenant with God to carry through this enterprise which they hoped would become like a city set on a hill, a model for others to follow.[26] A colony thus conceived would be no asylum for all who chose to come, but a carefully selected company of persons fit for the work in hand and sympathetic with its aims, or at least not antagonistic to them. Therefore, as Winthrop said a few years later, it was proper to reject as members of such a community persons "whose dispositions suite not with ours." [27]

When Winthrop's company arrived in Boston, there were already on the shores of the Bay persons who had no interest in the religious aims of the newcomers. Even among those who came out under the auspices of the Massachusetts Bay Company, not all were deeply concerned with the proposed Bible commonwealth. Assuming, then, the soundness of the ideals upheld by the leaders, it was natural and logical that an essential and first step in their program should be protection against

[25] A. B. Hart, *American History Told by Contemporaries*, I, 371.
[26] Text reproduced in Miller and Johnson, *The Puritans*, 195–199.
[27] *Ibid.*, "A Defence of an Order of Court" (1637), 199 ff.

hostile or indifferent elements. So the colony early limited settlement to persons "allowed by some of the Magistrates." Even with this selective process, further safeguards were thought necessary, including the restriction of the suffrage. The very small number of freemen, or fully qualified voters, of the Company who emigrated had to be increased, but not so far as to endanger the objectives of the promoters. Accordingly, the General Court, or legislature of the colony, limited the voting privilege to church members. The full effect of this restriction can be understood only if it is remembered that Puritan tests for church membership were so exacting that many religious persons, even among those in general sympathy with the doctrine and discipline of the Congregational churches, remained, voluntarily or otherwise, outside of the fold. These measures involved in themselves a decided concentration of power; but an attempt was made to carry the selective process still further.

According to the charter, the whole body of freemen sat with the governor, deputy governor, and assistants to legislate for the colony. For a short time this latter official group undertook to keep the authority in its own hands and even to impose a tax. This procedure, in direct violation of the charter, provoked a vigorous protest and was soon abandoned. Winthrop and his supporters subsequently won a partial victory by securing the division of the General Court into two houses. In this way the governor and assistants were able to veto action by the lower house, which now consisted of representatives from the towns. The net result was a political constitution extremely favorable to the leaders who desired the close coöperation of church and state, in the interest of what they conceived to be an ideal Christian society. In carrying through such a program, the influence of the clergy, a vigorous group of educated men, largely university graduates, was of course an important factor.

The proper relation between church and state, as seen from

the ecclesiastical point of view, was set forth in the Cambridge Platform adopted in 1648 by a synod of the Massachusetts churches. In general accord with Calvin's teaching, the church and the magistracy had their special fields of action, within which they were to act in accordance with the divine law as revealed in the Scriptures. Church officers should not meddle with the "Sword of the Magistrate" and the magistrate should not "meddle with the work proper to church officers"; the state should not, for instance, make church membership compulsory, thus bringing "unworthie ones in to the sanctuaries"; nor concern itself with "things meerly inward." Nevertheless, coöperation was expected. The magistrate, though primarily concerned with the second table of the Decalogue, that is to say, with a man's duties to his fellowmen, was also bound to promote the good life of the community "in matters of godliness." It was the business of the civil authorities to use their coercive power to punish "contempt of the word preached," "Idolatry, Blasphemy, Heresy, venting corrupt and pernicious opinions that destroy the foundation." Intervention by the civil authorities was also justifiable when any church became "schismatical." Thus, while the Congregational theory of church government was based on the independence of the local congregation, this freedom was by no means absolute.[28]

The position of the civil government as authoritatively stated in the *Lawes and Libertyes*, published by order of the General Court, was not essentially different.[29] This code, however, illustrates the willingness of the Puritans to entrust substantial power to the civil magistrate, when they could count on such authority being exercised by orthodox persons. The introduction emphasizes the advantages of isolation, which enabled the colony to build the state, as well as the churches,

[28] "Cambridge Platform" in Walker, *Creeds and Platforms of Congregationalism.*
[29] *The Book of the General Lawes and Libertyes*, 5, 6.

in accordance with the Scriptures. A curious illustration of this point is the section of the *Lawes and Libertyes* devoted to the listing of capital offenses. Supporting each penal clause are references—one or more—to the Mosaic code. Churches might be formed freely, provided their members were "orthodox in judgment"; but this must be done with the knowledge and approval of the magistrates, as well as of the neighboring clergy. Only members of a congregation so approved might qualify as voters. Each church might choose its own officers; but again with the qualification that they "be able, pious and orthodox." The church might discipline civil officers "in a church way," but ecclesiastical censure should not carry with it removal from public office. Conversely, the state might deal with any member or officer of the church "in a way of civil justice." There was also a comprehensive assignment of responsibility to the civil authority, "to see the peace, ordinances and rules of Christ be observed in everie church, according to his word." [30]

So much for general principles; how were they applied in practice? First, what did the church get out of its partnership with the commonwealth? Very much, certainly: the monopoly of public worship in the approved Congregational churches; the limitation of political privileges through the church-membership qualification for voting; the support of churches and their ministers by local taxation; and compulsory attendance on church services. To secure due respect for the clergy, there were penalties for disparaging ministers and their preaching; for a second offense, the offender had to pay a fine of five pounds or be publicly exhibited with a placard on his breast marking him as "An Open and Obstinate Contemner of God's Holy Ordinances." [31] In return for such support to the churches, the state could generally count on the

[30] *Ibid.*, 18–20.
[31] *Ibid.*, 19, 20.

help of the clergy against radical or subversive elements.[32] The satisfaction of both members in this partnership was well expressed by the Reverend John Cotton, the chief exponent of the ministerial point of view: "That government, which by the blessing of Christ, doth safely, speedily, and effectually purge out such grievous and dangerous evils, as threaten the ruine of Church and State, that government is safely allowed, and justly and wisely established in any civil State." [33]

We need not here repeat in detail the familiar story of the dealings of the Bay Commonwealth with dissentients from the "standing order," as seen in the cases of Roger Williams, Anne Hutchinson with her fellow-Antinomians, the Presbyterians, and the Quakers. For our present purpose, these episodes are chiefly significant, first as illustrating the coöperation of church and state in the procedure of prosecution and judgment; and, secondly, because in the case of Williams, particularly, the whole church-state theory of the Bay Colony was definitely challenged. Let us consider, first, the coöperative procedure. At the session of the General Court which ordered the banishment of Williams, all the clergy of the colony were called in for consultation, and when sentence was passed it was approved by all but one of the ministers.[34] In the so-called Antinomian controversy, the views of Anne Hutchinson and her associates were condemned by a church synod and Mrs. Hutchinson was excommunicated; but she was tried and banished by the civil authorities.

When Dr. Child and other sympathizers with the Presbyterian party in England asked for more liberal admission to church membership and consequently to the suffrage, the clergy were again consulted, though the fining and imprison-

[32] Cf. Miller, *Orthodoxy in Massachusetts*, chap. VII.

[33] *The Way of the Congregational Churches Cleared*, quoted in Miller, *Orthodoxy in Massachusetts*, 262.

[34] Hosmer, ed., *Winthrop's Journal*, I, 154, 162–163.

ment of Child for attempting an appeal to Parliament were determined by the civil authorities, and largely on the ground that such an appeal threatened the political independence of the colony.[35] The prosecution of the Quakers was pressed by the clergy, led by John Norton, a Boston pastor; but the legislation, which in its final form included the death penalty for those who returned after banishment, was enacted by the General Court and enforced by the magistrates. Aside from these more familiar cases, in which political as well as religious considerations were involved, Catholic priests were excluded, on pain of death if they returned. Anabaptists were to be banished as "Incendiaries of Commonwealths and the Infectors of persons in main matters of Religion"; and a general statute of 1646 imposed the same penalty for advocating "any damnable heresie." [36]

It was Roger Williams who most definitely challenged the Massachusetts doctrine that the state might take cognizance of errors in religion. It is well known that he incurred the hostility of the authorities on various grounds, including his extreme separatism, his criticism of Massachusetts land titles, and his objection to the taking of an oath by an "unregenerate man." In Winthrop's summing up of the case against him, these were all listed; but the first count in the indictment was his assertion that magistrates could not rightly punish offenses against the first table of the Decalogue, or in other words, strictly spiritual offenses. On this point, Williams's thinking was clarified in the course of his controversy with Cotton, of which more will be said later. Meantime, the prevailing theory in early Massachusetts was vigorously expressed in these often quoted words of Reverend Nathaniel Ward of Ipswich: "He that is willing to tolerate any Religion, or discrepant way of Religion, beside his owne, unlesse it be in matters meerly in-

[35] Miller, *Orthodoxy in Massachusetts*, 298–306.
[36] *Lawes and Libertyes*, I, 2, 24, 26.

different, either doubts of his owne, or is not sincere in it." [37] Incidentally, it may be added that Ward quoted with approval the famous saying of St. Augustine: *"Nullum malum pejus libertate errandi."*

In two important matters, Puritan New England assigned to the state functions then commonly assumed by the church. Marriage was treated as a civil contract rather than a sacrament, and the ceremony was at first performed by a magistrate instead of a minister. In education also the state assumed the primary responsibility. The Massachusetts system of elementary and grammar schools was established by the General Court and the duty of maintaining them was assigned to the town governments. Religion was certainly an important consideration in the Puritan scheme of education, but the Massachusetts schools were *state* schools. In the case of Harvard College, where religion was again an important though not the sole consideration, the institution was founded by the state, and its governing body included with six clergymen the governor, deputy governor, and all the magistrates.

No attempt is made here to treat in detail the politico-ecclesiastical situation in the other New England colonies. Rhode Island's "livelie experiment" of separating the church from the state will be considered later, and the case of Plymouth has already been noted. Of the two remaining members of the New England Confederation, New Haven, during less than a quarter century of independent existence was, if possible, more extreme in its theocracy than Massachusetts, while Connecticut differed less from Massachusetts than has often been supposed. Though its clerical leader, Thomas Hooker, was somewhat more democratic than Winthrop and his associates, his liberalism has been exaggerated. It was Hooker who was assigned by the Massachusetts authorities to convert

[37] "The Simple Cobbler of Aggawam in America," in Miller and Johnson, *The Puritans*, 230.

Roger Williams from the error of his ways; in most respects he was "thoroughly orthodox" in religion and politics.[38] Hooker's lay associate, John Haynes, the first governor of Connecticut, presided over the General Court which banished Williams and summed up the case against him.[39] To quote Professor Andrews, there was in the founding of Connecticut "no question of religious freedom" and "no intention of establishing a religious colony in any way different from that of Massachusetts." [40]

The Fundamental Orders drawn up by the Connecticut River towns in 1639 was a thoroughly Puritan document. Its declared purpose was not only to preserve public order, but to maintain "the liberty and purity of the Gospell" and "the disciplyne of the Churches." Though there was no formal church-membership qualification for the suffrage, the governor had to be a member of "some approved congregation." The Congregational churches were quite as definitely established here as in Massachusetts. After the coming of the Quakers, Connecticut joined the other colonies of the Confederation in legislation against them; they were forbidden to settle in the colony or to hold public meetings. While Connecticut policy in this, as in other respects, was not essentially different from that of Massachusetts, it was less harshly applied;[41] in the application of the death penalty to Quakers, Massachusetts stood alone.

We may conclude, then, that during a century and a half of European colonization in the Americas, European ideas of church and state were actually transplanted to the New World. This was substantially true of Catholic America—Spanish and French—of New Netherland, and of nearly all the English

[38] Miller and Johnson, *The Puritans*, 291.

[39] Osgood, *American Colonies in the Seventeenth Century*, I, 233, 291.

[40] Andrews, *The Colonial Period of American History*, II, 82.

[41] Greene, *Religious Liberty in Connecticut*, 165 ff.

colonies. So far as the latter group was concerned, there were in 1660 only two Continental colonies, numbering hardly a tenth of the English colonial population, in which church and state were not closely associated.[42] Generally speaking, in colonial America it was the accepted duty of the state to foster not merely religion in general, or Christianity in general, but a particular form of Christian faith and polity. Furthermore, the acceptance of this responsibility usually involved the suppression, if not always of dissenting *opinions*, at least of public worship other than that by law established.

[42] There were also Anglican establishments in the British West Indies.

III

Liberalizing Factors in Colonial America

WE HAVE seen that during more than a century and a half of
European settlement in the Americas, Old World attitudes in
matters of church and state were generally reflected in colonial
institutions. During the next century, no fundamental change
in this respect took place in Spanish and French America; it
was otherwise in the English colonies. There a variety of influences—idealistic principles along with thoroughly realistic
considerations of practical expediency—produced before the
close of the colonial era a radically different situation. During
this interval the movement toward religious liberty and
equality, though not wholly successful, did at least make substantial progress. In our study of this liberalizing development
we must first go back to Roger Williams and the founding of
Rhode Island. Though not the first colony to practise a policy
of toleration, it is of special interest from the standpoint of
theory.

In banishing Williams, the rulers of Massachusetts were
influenced by various considerations; certainly one count in
the indictment against him was his doctrine of the two tables
It was, said Williams, the business of the civil magistrate to
enforce the injunctions of the second table which concerned
man's dealings with his fellow men; but the punishment of
offenses against the first table, governing one's relations with
God, was not within the proper sphere of the state. After Williams left Massachusetts, the eccentricities which at first con-
fused his case gradually fell into the background and the

really important element in his thought could be seen in better perspective. As compared with most of his Puritan neighbors, Williams was an extreme separatist, not only in his insistence on the duty of separation from the Church of England because of its corruptions, but also in the sense in which the term is used by some modern writers on the history of religious liberty, to designate those who believe that religious liberty can best be secured by eliminating any intervention of the state in ecclesiastical affairs.

In the debate between Williams and John Cotton one sees a change of perspective as the discussion proceeded. Answering Cotton's defense of the Massachusetts authorities on the ground that the young radical was a disturber "both of civill and holy peace," [1] Williams still devoted most of his argument to a defense of separatism, in the narrower sense of refusing communion with churches that included unregenerate persons in their membership. Even then, however, he rose above this lower level in the latter part of his argument. The power of the magistrate must, he repeated, be limited to matters concerning "the Bodies and Goods, and outward state of men"; with the worship of God "and the consciences of men" he must not meddle. In any case, such intervention of the state in matters of faith did not pay, as the Religious Wars had shown. The confounding of church and state brought "all the world into Combustion." [2]

During the early years of the Rhode Island settlements, Williams twice visited England—once in the midst of the Civil War and again on the eve of Cromwell's protectorate, when the Presbyterian and Independent parties were actively debating the issue of toleration. The New England debate was thus brought into connection with that in the mother country; and the Williams-Cotton controversy produced three

[1] *Publications of the Narragansett Club*, I, 298.
[2] *Ibid.*, 313–396, especially 325, 335.

notable pamphlets, all printed in England: the first, by Williams, was entitled *The Bloudy Tenent of Persecution for cause of Conscience, discussed, in a Conference between Truth and Peace.* Cotton replied with *The Bloudy Tenent Washed and made White in the bloude of the Lambe;* and was followed by Williams's rejoinder, *The Bloudy Tenent yet more Bloudy by Mr. Cotton's Endeavour to wash it white in the Bloude of the Lambe.*

Though Cotton claimed that Massachusetts was not really guilty of persecution, he justified penal action against one who persisted in heresy after his error had been clearly shown and he had been duly admonished. In such a case, Cotton argued, the offender was "not persecuted for Cause of Conscience, but for sinning against his Owne Conscience." [3] Williams now showed himself at his best, discussing fundamental issues in a large way. Holding that compulsion in matters of conscience was essentially un-Christian, he met squarely the historic argument for persecution—that corrupt doctrine imperiled men's souls here and hereafter. That, he said, was doubtless true; but whatever the guilt involved, sentence could be pronounced only by the Divine Judge in the church; his "spirituall judicature," to be executed here and in eternity. "Such a sentence no Civill Judge can passe; such a death no Civill sword can inflict." Heresy must be fought, but only with spiritual weapons.[4] In his plea for religious liberty, Williams admitted no reservations; even "Popish and Jewish consciences" should be respected.[5]

In his general theory of the nature of the church, Williams departed widely not only from Catholic teaching but from that of most Protestants. Rejecting the idea of the church as the expression of the religious ideals of the community as a

[3] *Mr. Cotton's Answer, ibid.,* III, 42.

[4] *Bloody Tenent of Persecution, ibid.,* III, 125–127.

[5] *The Bloody Tenent Yet More Bloody, ibid.,* IV, 8, 47.

whole—whether international, national, or local—he regarded it as simply a voluntary association of individuals united by similar ideas of faith and worship. Though a thoroughgoing individualist in his defense of religious liberty, Williams insisted that he was no anarchist. As he put the case in his well-known letter to the town of Providence (1655), a ship at sea with its crew and passengers—"Papists" and Protestants, Jews and Turks—was "a true picture of a commonwealth." None of this company should be forced to attend the ship's services, or be disturbed in their own "particular prayers or worship"; but in directing the ship's course and preserving good order, the captain might properly enforce obedience upon all aboard.[6]

That Williams was ready to practise what he preached and was able to carry most of his associates with him is shown by the early history of the colony of which he was a principal founder. In the plantation covenant of the Providence settlers, obedience to the state was expressly limited to "civill things." [7] The neighboring island settlement also agreed that in its democratic government none should be "accounted a Delinquent for Doctrine: Provided, it be not directly repugnant to the government or lawes established." [8] The fidelity of the Rhode Islanders to these principles was severely tested by the hostility of their neighbors, who excluded them from the New England Confederation, and also by the coming of the Quakers. Williams's dislike of the latter was shown in his tract entitled *George Fox digg'd out of his Burrowes*, which Fox called "a very wicked and envious book." [9] Nevertheless, when called on by the Confederation to enact penal legislation against the Quakers, Rhode Island steadily refused. It was

[6] *Ibid.*, VI, 278–279.

[7] *Early Records of the Town of Providence* (Providence, 1892), I, 1.

[8] *Records of the Colony of Rhode Island*, I, 112–113.

[9] Quoted in Andrews, *Colonial Period*, II, 20 note.

admitted that Quaker doctrines, "if generally received," tended "to the very absolute cutting doune and overturninge relations and civill government among men"; but the colony had no law for punishing people because of their utterances "concerning the things and ways of God, as to salvation and an eternal condition." [10]

It was a notable event in the history of religious liberty when the British Crown gave its consent to Rhode Island's "livelie experiment" in the royal charter of 1663. Approving the purpose of that experiment, to show that the welfare of the state would be promoted by a "full libertie in religious concernements," the charter declared that no person in the colony should be called in question on account of his religious opinions, if he did not "actually disturb the civill peace." [11] Throughout the seventeenth century, Rhode Island seems to have acted in accord with this policy. Later, however, the record was marred by an enactment of uncertain date which limited citizenship and eligibility for public office to Protestant Christians. This law was not always strictly enforced and some Jews and Catholics were actually admitted to citizenship by special acts of the assembly; but in 1762 the Superior Court of the colony enforced the restrictive law by refusing the applications of two Jews for citizenship. There was, however, no penal legislation against either Catholics or Jews; and the latter were sufficiently numerous in Newport to maintain a synagogue.[12]

Though in the case of Rhode Island genuine religious conviction on the part of the founders was a prime factor in their policy of toleration, the charter shows that other influences

[10] *Records of the Colony of Rhode Island*, I, 376–378.

[11] *Ibid.*, II, 5.

[12] See S. S. Rider, "Inquiry Into the Origin of the Clause in the Laws of Rhode Island, 1719–1783, Disqualifying Roman Catholics," in *Rhode Island Historical Tracts*, 2d series, No. 1.

were at work in the same direction. Though the existing government in England was responsible for much intolerant legislation against dissenters, it was believed that such differences might be overlooked in a remote colony. It was also good policy to encourage a community whose prosperity seemed likely to advance the trade of the Empire. It is significant that the decade of the Rhode Island charter was also that of the Acts of Trade, or navigation laws, which aimed to exploit more effectively the economic resources of the colonies. Furthermore, the Restoration period was marked by the efforts of influential individuals to share in such exploitation through the acquisition of proprietary rights in new provinces. Both these developments contributed to the progress of religious toleration on this side of the Atlantic.

Let us consider first the proprietary system in its bearing on church and state relations. The institution of such governments by the Crown was not new; but of the earlier grants on the mainland, the only survivor in 1660 was Lord Baltimore's province of Maryland. Twenty-five years later at the death of Charles II, there were six proprietary governments in active operation on the Continent—New York, East New Jersey, West New Jersey, Pennsylvania, Maryland, and Carolina, covering together more territory along the seaboard than New England and Virginia combined. In all these provinces-governmental policies in relation to religion were radically different from those prevailing either in New England or Virginia. It was in the new proprietorships, and especially in Pennsylvania, that the most rapid growth of population took place in the next hundred years. The ecclesiastical policies of the proprietary governments are therefore of prime importance.

The distinguishing mark of the proprietorships was their feudal or semifeudal association of land ownership with governmental authority. The holders of such grants were real-estate promoters on a grand scale; they were also responsible for the maintenance of orderly governments in their respective territories. The history of the proprietary provinces is therefore largely concerned with the interaction between the landlord-tenant relation and that of ruler to subject. As landlords, the proprietors needed settlers who would raise profitably exportable products and provide revenue from quitrents. Concessions, political or economic, had to be made to prospective tenants, and it was obviously not good business to set up religious tests to exclude otherwise desirable immigrants. So it was that the proprietors tried to attract settlers by promising, if not full religious equality, at least greater tolerance than was allowed elsewhere. Among the prospective colonists to whom such privileges would appeal were members of dissenting groups in England, in Continental Europe, and in other colonies. Thus Puritan New Englanders who wished to better themselves were offered freedom to maintain in the new settlements local churches of the kind to which they had been accustomed.

In some proprietary enterprises the distinctly religious motive was not largely influential; in other provinces, as in Maryland and Pennsylvania, the desire of the proprietor to provide a refuge for a particular religious group certainly had an important part. In the case of Maryland, the original promoter, Sir George Calvert, first Lord Baltimore, and his son, Cecilius, the actual recipient of the charter, were both Catholics, members of a persecuted minority in England and debarred from political careers because of their conversion to the old faith. It was largely to provide an asylum for Catholics and opportunities for Catholic missions among the Indians that the colony was undertaken. Comparatively few persons of that faith, however, desired to leave their homes where life seemed endurable in spite of intermittently enforced fines for failure to attend Anglican services; so from the start Protestants, as well as Catholics, were recruited for the colony. On this point we have the statement of Charles Calvert, the third Lord Baltimore, who was also for a time the resident governor of the province. There were many, he said, who were willing to go as colonists, "soe as they might have a Generall Toleration . . . by a Lawe by which all of all sorts who professed Christianity in Generall might be at liberty to worshipp God in such manner as was most agreeable with their respective Judgments and Consciences . . . without the complying with these conditions in all probability, This Provynce had never beene planted." [13] The charter contained no clear reference to the religion of the proprietor, any more than the Massachusetts charter referred to Puritans, nor is there anything about toleration of diverse faiths. Instead, the proprietor was authorized to erect churches and other places of worship, of which he was to be the patron, with the understanding that they were to be dedicated and consecrated according to the ecclesiastical laws of England.[14]

In establishing his colony, Lord Baltimore had a difficult situation to deal with. In England, the Puritan party called for rigorous enforcement of the penal legislation against "Popish recusants"; and the Maryland settlement had not gone far before the Civil War began, followed by Puritan control of the English government. Across the Potomac from the new province was Virginia, from whose territory Maryland had been taken. The Virginians not only resented this loss but many of them were strongly anti-Catholic. Under these circumstances, Lord Baltimore displayed a high order of practical statesmanship, keeping an even hand between Catholics and Protestants and cautioning his fellow churchmen against antagonizing their Protestant neighbors. Like other rulers of his time, whether Catholic or Protestant, Lord Baltimore was jealous of his prerogatives as the head of the civil government.

[13] *Archives of Maryland*, V, 267–268.
[14] English translation in Hall, *Narratives of Early Maryland*.

Thus he insisted, in accordance with the English law of mortmain, that conveyances of land to the missionaries were not valid without his consent. This and other issues between the proprietor and the Maryland clergy were settled in his favor with the approval of the ecclesiastical authorities in Europe.

A fair judgment of Lord Baltimore's toleration policy must rest largely on his own administration and that of his agents during the period when he was comparatively, though not wholly, free to develop his own policy. The famous Act of Toleration of 1649 can be fully understood only in its political setting. Malcontents in the colony, aided by Baltimore's enemies in Virginia, caused such disorder that his deputy governor had for a time to leave the province. Meantime, civil war raged in England, with the Puritan party finally victorious. Under these circumstances, Baltimore tried to allay the excitement by appointing a Protestant governor, whose oath of office required him not to disturb any one "professing to beleeve in Jesus Christ," in the free exercise of his religion, "and in particular no Roman Catholick." [15] This action was followed by Baltimore's proposal of "An Act Concerning Religion," which was adopted with additions by the Maryland Assembly. From an ideal standpoint, this act left much to be desired. Its primary purpose was to make possible the peaceable living together of Catholics and Protestants, believers in those Christian tenets on which orthodox persons in both camps could agree, including the doctrine of the Trinity. Lord Baltimore was probably not responsible for the appalling provision of the law imposing the death penalty for the denial of that doctrine, and it does not seem ever to have been applied. In view of actual conditions in England, much was gained by this promise of mutual toleration between Catholics and Protestants. The dominant purpose of maintaining peaceful relations between these two groups is illus-

[15] The oath in Hall, *Narratives of Early Maryland*, 212–214.

trated by the penalties imposed for the use of abusive epithets by either party, as for instance such terms as heretics and schismatics applied by Catholics to Protestants, and others applied by Protestants to Catholics, such as "Idolator," "popish priest," and "Jesuited papist." [16]

Arrayed against the proprietary government were the Puritan settlers, many of them newcomers from Virginia who had found refuge there from repressive measures in that colony, their sympathizers in Virginia, and, finally, commissioners appointed by the parliamentary authorities in England. This combination proved for a time too strong for Lord Baltimore and his supporters, and his government was overthrown. Thereupon the victorious Puritans passed their own act on religion, which denied religious liberty both to Catholics and Anglicans. This insurgent government was, however, short-lived. Cromwell's government now supported Lord Baltimore, and the restored proprietary government revived the Act of Toleration. It remained in force until the Revolution of 1689, when Maryland became for a time a royal province.

Of the later proprietary governments, the most significant for the history of religious liberty was that of William Penn. For him the founding of Pennsylvania was not only a business enterprise but a "holy experiment," conceived in a liberal, yet distinctly religious, spirit. Long before he received his charter, Penn had been active both as a leader among the Friends and as an ardent advocate of toleration. No merely theoretical defender of religious liberty, he had known what it was to suffer imprisonment in defense of his principles. In one of his early writings, *The Great Case of Liberty of Conscience* . . . *Briefly Debated and Defended* (1670), he opposed coercion in matters of conscience as not only unreasonable but un-Christian; to quote his own words, "imposition, restraint and persecution for conscience sake, highly invade the Divine pre-

[16] *Archives of Maryland*, I, 244–247.

rogative." [17] Again, in a letter to the Duke of Ormond, he wrote: "Let the tares grow with the wheat, errors of judgment remain till removed by the power of light and conviction . . . For my part, I frankly declare that I can not think that God will damn any man for the errors of his judgment." [18] Since the Quakers looked to the "inner light" of the Christian conscience as the ultimate authority, rather than an infallible Bible or an infallible church, they could not consistently take any other stand.

Penn had his first opportunity to apply his principles in the actual management of a colony when he became one of the Quaker proprietors of West New Jersey. Their Concessions and Agreements (1677), for which Penn was largely responsible, denied the right of any person or persons "to rule over Men's Consciences in Religious matters"; no one in this province should suffer in any way because of his faith or mode of worship.[19] The royal grant of Pennsylvania to Penn as sole proprietor naturally offered a much wider opportunity for the development of his ideas. Soon afterward, he set down as "the first fundamentall" of his government freedom of faith and worship "in such way and manner as every Person shall in conscience beleive is most acceptable to God." [20] Under the Great Law enacted in 1682 and substantially in accord with Penn's ideas, no person who acknowledged one God and agreed to live "peaceably and justly under the civil government" was to be disturbed because of his religious faith and worship or compelled to attend any service other than that of his own choice. Penn and his friends were not, however, secularists in their ideas of government. Sunday observance

[17] Penn, *Select Works* (London, 1782), III, 9 ff.

[18] Quoted in Sharpless, *Quaker Experiment in Government*, I, 118.

[19] Andrews, *Colonial Period*, III, 167; *New Jersey Archives*, I, 253.

[20] "Fundamental Constitutions" in *Pennsylvania Magazine of History and Biography*, XX, 286.

was required with rest from "common toil," and this not merely for "the ease of the creation," but in order to prevent the growth of "Looseness, irreligion and Atheism . . . under pretence of Conscience"; there should be time for reading the Scriptures either at home or in such place of public worship as each person might prefer. Though freedom of faith and worship was guaranteed to all believers in God, thus including the Jews, political privileges were limited to Christians. There were also penalties for profanity.[21] In short, Penn's commonwealth was meant to be a Christian society, but without enforced conformity. This tolerant policy was reasserted in the Charter of Privileges, which he issued in 1701.

The maintenance of Penn's policies proved to be difficult. Under pressure from the British government, and with the final acquiescence of the Quaker colonists, Catholics were excluded from public office. It is only fair, however, to remember that on the eve of the Revolution Pennsylvania was the only one of the thirteen colonies in which the services of the Roman communion were publicly held. On two other issues Quaker principles came into conflict with the demands of the home government. The refusal of conscientious Friends to bear arms or support warlike measures, including the passage of militia acts and the appropriation of money for defense, resulted in long and acrimonious controversies. Individual Quakers were not actually compelled to bear arms, but their representatives in the colonial assembly were seriously embarrassed, with the result that in the crisis of the last French war most of them solved the problem by giving up their seats. In the matter of oaths, the Quakers were similarly embarrassed. Colonial acts allowing the substitution of affirmations in all cases, instead of with certain exceptions as under the English law, were disallowed by the Crown. In the end,

[21] *Charter to William Penn and Laws of the Province of Pennsylvania,* 107–109.

affirmation was permitted for all purposes, but a Quaker judge might be called upon to take part in proceedings requiring the administration of oaths to persons who did not share his scruples. In this dilemma some of the Friends adjusted themselves to the situation; yet the Society held firm on the principle and its more conscientious members refrained from service on the bench.[22]

Though the idealist element in Penn's policies was certainly important, his concern for the economic prosperity of the province and his own stake in the enterprise cannot be ignored. His widely advertised proposals to settlers, including the promise of religious liberty, brought immigrants from the Continent as well as from the British Isles, thus making possible a more rapid growth in population than in any of the older colonies. Penn's hope of substantial profits from the province was not realized, and he was so much embarrassed financially that he was on the point of giving up his proprietorship. Nevertheless, he left a valuable inheritance to his sons. Furthermore, the prosperity of a province that welcomed settlers of many different creeds undoubtedly made for tolerant policies elsewhere.

In the plans of other proprietors—those of Carolina and New York, and the original grantees of New Jersey—religious considerations were less important than the profit motive. They served the cause of toleration, however, by using it as an inducement to prospective settlers. The proprietors of Carolina, two of whom also acquired New Jersey from the Duke of York, were Church of England men—several of them leading members of the Stuart government which was responsible for extremely harsh legislation against dissenters. Nevertheless, they needed settlers if their American estates were to have any value; anyhow, the framers of the charter

[22] Sharpless, *Quaker Experiment in Government*, I, 136–148; Root, *Relations of Pennsylvania with the British Government*, chaps. VIII–X.

hoped that "by reason of the remote distance of these places" there would be "no breach of the unity and uniformity established in this nation." So, exercising their privilege of granting toleration to settlers, the Carolina proprietors made successful efforts to attract Puritan settlers from New England and elsewhere. Though the Church of England was legally established, New Englanders and other dissenters were not only accorded freedom of conscience in the restricted sense but permitted to form congregations with ministers of their own choice.[23]

Similar action was taken by the proprietary government of New York and the first proprietors of New Jersey, with the result that in all these colonies dissenters became numerous and in the end far outnumbered the adherents of the Church of England. In New Jersey, where the original proprietors sold their rights, their successors in East and West Jersey included, with the Quakers, representatives of several other religious groups. So it came about that there was no established church in either of the Jerseys.

The position of the Duke of York in the former Dutch province of New Netherland was somewhat different. He himself, though not a publicly professing Catholic at first, was an acknowledged member of that church during the greater part of his proprietorship. Adherents of the Church of England were few, chiefly officials, including the chaplain of the garrison. The overwhelming majority of the inhabitants were English or Dutch Calvinists, although, as under the Dutch regime, there were several other small religious groups, among them a few Catholics. Under such conditions, a church establishment could at best be merely nominal; the liberties of the Dutch church had been definitely guaranteed by the Eng-

[23] Charter of 1663 in *Colonial Records of North Carolina*, I, 32; cf. "Concessions and Agreements," 1665, *ibid.*, 79–81; "Fundamental Constitutions," *ibid.*, 203.

lish when the province was surrendered. Accordingly, the new government, under the so-called Duke's Laws, granted toleration to all Protestant congregations whose ministers could show that they had been regularly ordained. In each community the dominant church, whether Anglican, Dutch Reformed, or English Puritan, might support its worship by local taxation;[24] as a matter of fact, the only Episcopal service during the whole proprietary period was that conducted by the Anglican army chaplain. The state supervised all the churches; but ordinarily the local congregations were left very much to themselves. Not until the last decade of the seventeenth century was the Church of England really established, even partially. Its members were still in a small minority and the establishment was limited to a few counties; even there it was not very effective.

In short, the proprietary regimes everywhere permitted a considerable degree of religious toleration, at least among Protestants; in early Maryland and in Pennsylvania, Catholic and Protestant worship went on side by side. Toleration having resulted in a multiplicity of sects, this variety in itself worked against the subsequent establishment of any one church, even when most of the proprietary provinces had been taken over by the Crown.

In the development of toleration, the home government itself had an important part, not only through the granting of proprietary charters but also in other ways. British statesmen might favor the extension of the Anglican system, but they were rarely willing to sacrifice any material political or economic interest for that purpose. Furthermore, they had no interest whatever in supporting the Puritan establishments of New England. In those colonies, where the Church of England itself was commonly regarded as no better than an un-

[24] "Duke of Yorke's Book of Laws" in *Charter to William Penn and Laws of the Province of Pennsylvania,* 18.

desirable dissenting sect, the home government became in fact an ally of the minority groups. The Andros regime in New England, which sharply curtailed the political privileges of the Puritan colonies, worked on the whole for religious liberty. It was under this autocratic government that Episcopal services were, for the first time, permitted in Boston.[25] When after the Revolution of 1688 the English government refused to reëstablish the old charter government, toleration, though not religious equality, was secured to all Protestants by the new province charter of 1691.

From 1660 on, the trend of British policy was in the same general direction, even in the royal provinces. One factor during the Restoration period was the religious position of the last two Stuarts. Both ultimately became Catholics, and even before formal conversion Charles II was sympathetic with his Catholic subjects. They naturally favored the repeal of the harsh legislation against members of that church; and this could hardly be brought about except by measures of toleration that would include Protestant dissenters as well as Catholics. In England this Stuart policy was defeated by a combination of Anglican churchmen with the main body of Puritans who feared the growth of Catholic influence, and the Revolution of 1688 drove James II from his throne. In the colonies the instructions to royal governors show a fairly liberal tendency, so far as religion was concerned, partly on economic grounds. Thus in 1679, the governor of Virginia was reminded that it was desirable to encourage the immigration of persons who might come to the province with their property, even though they were of "different persuasions in matters of religion." Such persons should be protected in the exercise of their religion, if they were peaceable, "not giving offense or scandal." In his own household, however, the

25 Viola Barnes, *Dominion of New England* (New Haven, 1923), chap. VI.

governor was to conform to the Anglican church, which he should also *recommend* to others.[26] During the next decade, royal instructions for Virginia, New England, and New York required the governor to allow liberty of conscience to all orderly persons; in New York, the governor in question, Thomas Dongan, was a Catholic. Reference may also be made here to the much later intervention of the British government to protect dissenters in South Carolina against Anglican intolerance and in Massachusetts against the Puritan regime.[27]

The English Revolution of 1688 brought another change of policy. Protestant dissenters, who had coöperated with Anglican churchmen in the Revolution, were rewarded by the Act of Toleration of 1689, which gave them the right to hold public services subject to the registration of their ministers and places of worship. The Church of England, however, retained its special privileges and dissenters were still disqualified for office by sacramental tests. Even from this grudging toleration, two religious groups were excluded. In the case of the Catholics, this action was largely on political grounds. The animosities excited by the arbitrary proceedings of James II had intensified anti-Catholic feeling; even so liberal a thinker as John Locke believed that Catholics owed an allegiance to the Papacy inconsistent with complete loyalty to the state. For other reasons, toleration was not promised to persons who denied the doctrine of the Trinity.[28]

Colonial policy in general followed the pattern of the English Act of Toleration. The Massachusetts charter of 1691, while providing for a royal governor and the royal disallowance of colonial statutes, left the established Congregational system substantially untouched, although it prom-

[26] Labaree, *Royal Instructions to Colonial Governors*, II, 495.
[27] *Ibid.*, 494-495.
[28] Robertson, *Select Statutes*, 70–75; J. Locke, *Letter on Toleration* (1689).

ised toleration for Protestant dissenters from that system, including Anglicans, Quakers, and Baptists. In this and other royal provinces, the Catholics gained nothing by either the English or colonial revolutions; in fact, they were sometimes worse off than before. In Virginia, for instance, the governor's instructions of 1685 required that liberty of conscience should be given to all orderly persons, but those of 1690 introduced the words "except Papists." In Maryland, when the overthrow of Lord Baltimore's government brought in a royal governor, the toleration policy of the Catholic proprietor was abandoned and the Church of England was established by law. Protestant dissenters were tolerated, but there was harsh penal legislation against the Catholics that remained on the statute books and was even extended after the proprietary government was restored to a Protestant heir of the Baltimore family. There was similar drastic legislation in New York and Massachusetts. In this respect, public opinion in most of the colonies at the close of the seventeenth century was quite in accord with that in England. So far as Protestants were concerned, the principle of toleration had made substantial gains, and the attempt to enforce uniformity of doctrine and worship had to be given up. Even among Protestants, however, there was discrimination in favor of the established churches, and nowhere did the small minority of Catholic inhabitants escape some form of discriminatory legislation.

Developments in the later colonial era must be summarized briefly. British and colonial regulation of immigration and naturalization either excluded Catholics or in one way or another discriminated against them, even, as we have seen, in Roger Williams's own colony of Rhode Island. Anti-Catholic feeling was, almost inevitably, kept alive and at times intensified by the intercolonial wars with the Catholic powers of France and Spain; in the North especially, the Jesuit missionaries were not only servants of the church but also good French patriots whose influence among the Indians was exerted in the interest of France. Nevertheless, the increasing variety of racial and religious elements, especially in the newly settled areas of the middle colonies and the South, gradually accustomed Americans to the possibility of living on at least tolerable terms with men who had different ideas of faith and worship from their own.

The French immigrant, St. John Crèvecœur, has in his *Letters from an American Farmer* a striking passage, which, though hardly to be taken literally, does suggest what was happening in many places. Crevecœur's hypothetical traveler, on a country road, passes first a Catholic "who prays to God as he has been taught" and whose "prayers offend nobody"; then, in succession, the farm of an "honest, plodding German Lutheran," a Scotch Presbyterian, a member of the Dutch Reformed Church; there might even be a Quaker meeting. If these people were honest, industrious, and peaceable, contacts between them were likely to bring tolerance of ecclesiastical differences or sometimes sheer indifference to such distinctions; there might even be intermarriage across denominational lines. With such mixed populations, enforced uniformity became increasingly difficult. Where there was no established church, the variety of religions formed an effective barrier against attempts to introduce one; where establishments existed, they were steadily weakened by the growing strength of dissenting groups.[29]

Two other general influences, quite different from each other and indeed mutually antagonistic, worked against both Anglican and Puritan establishments—the Great Awakening and the extension to the New World of eighteenth-century rationalism, either in the form of deism or of latitudinarian tendencies in the Christian churches. The Great Awakening,

[29] J. Hector St. John [Crèvecœur], *Letters from an American Farmer* (ed. Belfast, 1783), 39–40.

associated with Jonathan Edwards, the New Light Presbyterian Tennents of the middle colonies, the Methodist George Whitefield, and also to some extent with German pietism, drew men of various antecedents toward a more personal and emotional religion than they had found in Anglican churches or Puritan meetinghouses. Regarded with suspicion by conservative clergy and laymen, this ardent evangelism found expression in new separatist churches among the Congregationalists of New England; in other colonies Presbyterians were divided between Old Side and New Side churches. Revivalism also brought recruits to the rising "popular churches," first to the Baptists and later, on the eve of the Revolution, to the Methodists. In general, these revivalist groups had no quarrel with traditional Christian theology; they were generally "fundamentalists," in our present-day meaning of that word. They gradually developed an effective opposition to the established churches. Whether themselves tolerant or intolerant, they resisted coercion and discrimination in favor of the standing order; in the case of the Baptists, especially, there was a European background of thoroughgoing separatism— of hostility to any association of church and state.

Meantime, a kind of "peaceful penetration" took place in the established churches themselves. Representative laymen like John Adams and Jefferson were in varying degrees moving away from orthodox theology, whether Anglican or Calvinist. Adams is a particularly good example of the inner revolution as distinguished from any frontal attack on the churches. He was, as he once put it, a "churchgoing animal," but quite out of sympathy with the "New England theology" of an earlier generation. Among the Congregational ministers of that period, Jonathan Mayhew is probably the best representative of the revolt from orthodox Calvinism, which later took the form of Unitarianism. Similar latitudinarian and skeptical tendencies appeared in Anglican communities among the clergy, and to a greater extent among the laity, as for instance in the circle of Jefferson's friends at Williamsburg. Madison is an interesting example of a Virginian who belonged to an Anglican family but whose college training in the North helped to liberalize his attitude toward dissent in his own province. Latitudinarianism in theology did not necessarily involve opposition to a moderate form of church establishment; but, by and large, it weakened the resistance of the established churches to the demands of dissenting minorities.

In Virginia, dissent won its first considerable victory with the passage of a provincial measure in 1699, which substantially applied the principle of the English statute of 1689.[30] Dissenting congregations whose meeting places and ministers were duly licensed could hold their public worship, though their numbers were too few in the tidewater to excite much antagonism. During the middle decades of the eighteenth century, the Presbyterians especially found their way into Virginia in increasing numbers. So long as they were largely confined to the back country and the Great Valley, the Church of England planters and their clergy were not seriously disturbed. As in the case of the proprietary provinces and that of the English government itself, it seemed good policy to attract immigrants to remote frontier areas by the promise of religious toleration. Such a promise was accordingly given by Governor Gooch of Virginia to the Presbyterian synod of Philadelphia.

Presently, however, the situation changed. Dissenters became more numerous east of the mountains, especially in the Piedmont country, and the New Light preachers of these later years were more aggressive than the early representatives of conservative northern Presbyterianism. The supporters of the establishment thereupon used the restrictive provisions of the Act of Toleration, regarding the registration of ministers and

[30] Hening, *Statutes of Virginia*, III, 171.

67

meeting places, to curb the New Light preachers, who had no fixed residence. Dissenters were fined and ministers were refused licenses. At this point, however, two factors combined to bring partial relief. One was the more liberal attitude of the English government. Following the advice of the royal attorney general, the Board of Trade warned the Virginia authorities against harsh treatment of dissenters; religious liberty was, in the opinion of the Board, "essential to the enriching and improving of a trading nation." [31] The other important factor in favor of toleration was the oncoming of the French and Indian War, when united action was needed for the defense of the province. So it came about that the Virginia Presbyterians enjoyed a substantial measure of toleration, side by side with the established church, though by no means on an equal footing; the obligation to pay tithes, for instance, was still applicable to dissenters as well as churchmen. The Baptists, now rapidly increasing in numbers, aroused more antagonism and on the eve of the Revolution suffered serious persecution.

In the South generally the number of dissenters increased steadily until they outnumbered the supporters of the Anglican church. At the end of the colonial era, the Church of England was still legally established in that section. It was in no condition, however, to defend itself when the support of the Crown was withdrawn and the old ruling class lost much of its power.

The standing order in New England was more strongly entrenched. In no way dependent on any external authority, it was supported by a much more homogeneous population, for immigration to this section was comparatively small. Even here, however, concessions had to be made. Quakers, Baptists, and Episcopalians had by the end of the seventeenth century

[31] Quoted in Osgood, *American Colonies in the Seventeenth Century,* III, 475.

won the right to maintain their own worship; yet they were still at a disadvantage, for they had to pay taxes to support Congregational ministers. Gradually, however, the dissenters gathered strength and secured some relief. In their fight against church taxes, they profited partly by their growing membership, which in the case of the Episcopalians owed something to the missionary efforts of the Church of England Society for Propagating the Gospel. So, under pressure from minority groups supported by sympathizers in England, both Massachusetts and Connecticut allowed duly certified members of dissenting congregations either exemption from church taxes or, as in the case of the Episcopalians, the right to have their local taxes applied to the support of their own clergy. In this respect New England dissenters were better off than Virginia Presbyterians and Baptists. It is worth noting that during this period the English Privy Council intervened to release dissenters who had been imprisoned for obstructing the assessment of church taxes.[32]

So matters stood on the eve of the Revolution. Church establishments of a sort existed in a majority of the thirteen colonies, but they were clearly losing ground. Furthermore, the prosperity of such colonies as Rhode Island and Pennsylvania, under their comparatively tolerant governments, had its influence elsewhere. Virginia attracted desirable settlers from Pennsylvania by offering toleration to frontier settlers, and Rhode Island proved a convenient base from which preachers went out to reinforce dissenting groups elsewhere in New England. In short, the time was ripe for more radical departures from the prevailing theory and practice of the early colonial era. The impact of revolution was soon to bring further advance in the same direction.

[32] Reed, *Church and State in Massachusetts*, 116–126.

IV

"Separation"

JUST how far religious partisanship affected the course of the
political controversy between Great Britain and the colonies—
to what extent it contributed to the psychology of discontent
and revolution—is a question that cannot be answered in any
mathematical fashion. Without claiming for religion a position
of primary importance in the progress of the Revolutionary
movement, it may safely be said that there were significant
relations between religion and politics during this period.
There is definite contemporary evidence for such relations in
the statements of radical Whigs and conservative Loyalists.

The connection was most evident in New England. In Feb-
ruary 1775, a "Gentleman on board the Fleet at Boston" sent
to his brother in London his impressions of the situation in this
neighborhood. "Mankind," he wrote, "in general are very
jealous of any innovation in their religion; of this the leaders
have taken the advantage, and impressed on the minds of the
people that the Romish [religion] is going to be established
in America by an act of Parliament, that they have begun with
Canada, and intend to introduce it among the rest of the Colonies. . . . In their churches, the Gospel is laid aside for
politics." [1] A few weeks earlier another writer from Boston

[1] M. W. Willard, *Letters on the American Revolution* (Boston,
Houghton, Mifflin Company, 1925), 67–68.

expressed a fairly common Loyalist view: "The inhabitants of New England are the descendants of Cromwell's *elect* and they not only inherit their sentiments in civil and religious matters, but they have copied after them during the contest they have had with the Mother Country." [2] In opposition to these subversive tendencies the adherents of the Church of England, from New England to Maryland, were said with some exaggeration to be "uniformly attached to Great Britain." On the Whig side one has only to turn the pages of Samuel Adams's correspondence to find numerous references to the impending danger from "prelacy and popery." Many years later John Adams recalled the important contributions made to the Revolutionary propaganda by three Boston ministers—Jonathan Mayhew, Charles Chauncy, and Samuel Cooper.[3] For numerous illustrations of the work of the Puritan clergy in popularizing the compact theory of government, so closely associated in their minds with the church covenants of the "New England way," the interested reader may turn to a recent study of *The New England Clergy and the American Revolution* by Alice Baldwin.

In New York, which had among its chief political leaders a substantial number of Yale graduates, the more radical group in provincial politics was commonly referred to as the "Presbyterian party." One of the outstanding Whigs of this region, William Livingston of the Yale Class of 1741, was also a leader among Presbyterian laymen, and as such participated in conferences held by the clergy of that denomination with their brethren of the Connecticut Consociation of Congregational churches. The best known Loyalist testimony to the Whiggish tendencies of the Presbyterians in the middle colonies is that of Joseph Galloway, the ablest leader of the Pennsylvania conservatives. The opposition to British authority was

[2] *Ibid.*, 12.
[3] *Works*, X, 271, 284.

in his opinion largely due to a combination of Congregationalists and Presbyterians;[4] although his highly colored picture of a republican conspiracy between these two denominations cannot be taken at its face value, it does represent fairly the attitude of many members of his party and contains a kernel of truth. Certain it is that in May 1775, as the Second Continental Congress was beginning its sessions, the Presbyterian Synod of New York and Philadelphia issued a pastoral letter urging vigorous support of this revolutionary assembly, though still professing loyalty to King George.[5] In the opinion of their most distinguished spokesman, John Witherspoon, president of the College of New Jersey, the union of the colonies against the Mother Country was founded on "a deep and general conviction" that religious, as well as civil, liberty depended on the issue of this conflict.[6]

In the South the situation was more complicated. In Virginia, for instance, where the Church of England had a century and a half of history behind it, it was deeply interwoven with the social texture of the tidewater country. It was natural enough, then, that while some of the most influential Anglican clergy were Loyalist, many others joined their parishioners in support of the Continental cause; several of them served as chaplains in the Continental army. Nevertheless the Presbyterians, largely of Ulster-Scottish origin, supplied more than their share of militant Whiggism. The Hanover Presbytery of this province recalled the hardships its members had suffered under the Anglican establishment and expressed the belief that, once relieved from British tyranny, the Assembly would "cheerfully concur in removing every species of reli-

[4] *Historical Reflections on the Rise and Progress of the American Revoltion* (London, 1780), 58.
[5] *Records of the Presbyterian Church in the United States of America* (Philadelphia, 1841), 466–469.
[6] *Works*, III, 36 (ed. Philadelphia, 1802).

gious, as well as civil bondage." [7] In the lower South there were other complicating circumstances that prevented a clean-cut alignment between churchmen and dissenters. In both groups there were ardent Whigs and conservative Loyalists. In the back country many good Scottish Presbyterians of comparatively recent immigration had their grievances against certain Whig leaders of the seaboard and remained loyal to the Crown.

In short, while sweeping generalizations are impossible, especially as regards the laymen of the Anglican communion, there was, as in England, a tendency among thoroughgoing churchmen to maintain the ancient association of throne and altar as against what they regarded as a revival of the republican and leveling tendencies of the seventeenth-century Puritan commonwealth. This tendency was reinforced, especially for the Northern clergy, by their dependence on the English Society for the Propagation of the Gospel in Foreign Parts.

The two issues that most definitely associated religion with politics during this period were, first, the renewal of an old effort to establish an Anglican episcopate in the colonies, and, second, the concessions made by the British government to the Catholic Church in Canada. On general principles, nothing seemed more reasonable than that the Anglican churches in America should be provided with resident bishops. There was certainly something anomalous in the position of an Episcopal Church without bishops nearer than three thousand miles away to administer the essential rites of confirmation and ordination. To members of other communions, however, the proposal appeared in a very different light. After all, the English bishops were not merely spiritual guides to their own flocks; they were also closely associated with the state, exercising functions that

[7] In Humphrey, *Nationalism and Religion*, 78–81, from Foote, *Sketches of Virginia*.

involved dissenters as well as churchmen. It was impossible for colonials brought up in the Puritan tradition to forget what their ancestors had suffered at the hands of seventeenth-century bishops and diocesan courts. In 1768, a writer in the *New York Post-Boy* argued that under the common law an American bishop might establish a diocesan court, "a tribunal ... which Americans dread to almost the same degree of horror which they feel at the thoughts of the Inquisition itself." [8] Furthermore, while supporters of the proposed American episcopate generally disavowed any desire to restrict the privileges of laymen and dissenters, the confidential correspondence of such leading churchmen as President Samuel Johnson of King's College shows that they hoped to win support in England by suggesting that an adequately organized church would prove useful in maintaining the just rights of the Crown.[9]

As a matter of fact, few English politicians were interested in the episcopate scheme. It was too unpopular with the English dissenters whose support was needed by the dominant party. The supposed danger to American dissenters and to religious liberty was really slight. Nevertheless the prominence given to this issue in New England indicates fairly widespread feeling which could be exploited by such revolutionary leaders as Samuel Adams in Massachusetts and William Livingston in New York. Even Virginia churchmen, clerical as well as lay, disliked the proposal.

Puritan attacks on the Anglican Church often assumed that "prelacy" and "popery" were closely related. For many Americans of this period the idea was strengthened by the Quebec Act of 1774, which was intended to solve certain problems in the administration of that lately conquered province.

[8] I. N. P. Stokes, *Iconography of Manhattan Island* (New York, 1928), IV, 784.

[9] Schneider, *Samuel Johnson*, I, 346, 359, 367.

The important feature of the Quebec Act, for our present discussion, was the provision that secured to the Catholic clergy the payment of tithes in accordance with the practice of the French regime. Protestants were definitely exempted, and the measure was, from an eighteenth-century standpoint, a reasonable fulfillment of the Treaty of 1763, by which Canada became a British province.[10] Nevertheless the bill was denounced as an establishment of the Catholic Church and as a menace to Protestantism in the other colonies. Violent declarations of this kind were general and were even echoed by the first Continental Congress in some of its state papers, notably in its "Address to the People of Great Britain." [11] According to this pronouncement, the Quebec Act was designed "to reduce the ancient free Protestant colonies to the same state of slavery" as that of the Canadians. Congress went on to express astonishment that Parliament should consent to establish in Canada a religion that had "deluged your island in blood, and dispersed impiety, bigotry, persecution, murder and rebellion throughout every part of the world." There was, however, some objection in Congress to such a statement.[12]

This survey of religion and politics in the prewar phase of the Revolution seems to justify a few general conclusions especially significant for our study of religion and the state. First of all, there was in the minds of many of the leaders a disposition to associate the struggle for civil liberty with that for religious freedom. By many supporters of the Puritan regime in Massachusetts this was commonly interpreted to mean freedom from interference with the old standing order by an episcopal jurisdiction which in their view would not be

[10] V. Coffin, *The Province of Quebec and the Early American Revolution* (Madison, 1896), 432–450; the text of the Act is pp. 544–552.

[11] *Journals of Congress* (ed. Library of Congress), I, 88.

[12] Duane's notes in E. C. Burnett, ed., *Letters of Members of the Continental Congress* (Washington, D. C., 1921), I, 77–79.

content with purely spiritual functions. As regards dissenters from the New England establishments, even so liberal a man as Franklin observed that existing concessions had already placed them in a much more favorable position than that of the English nonconformists. Against this restricted view of religious liberty, however, Massachusetts Baptists and Quakers were already protesting under the leadership of such men as the Baptist minister, Isaac Backus. The protests of these New England minorities, though for the moment disregarded, pointed the way toward more liberal policies in the future. More consistent than the Puritan position was that of the Virginia Presbyterians and Baptists who opposed any form of religious establishment. The Presbytery of Hanover in that province declared, in 1776, that official preference to any Christian denomination implied a "claim to infallibility" comparable with that of the Church of Rome. "Therefore," they said, "we ask no establishment for ourselves; neither can we approve of them when granted to others." [13]

So far, however, majority opinion, as expressed by local and Continental declarations, conceived of religious equality as something to be applied within the limits of Protestant Christianity. Catholicism was condemned not only as "superstitious," but as involving obligations to "a foreign potentate," which would be inconsistent with loyalty to the commonwealth.

With the actual outbreak of war, however, there came important changes in the American outlook. The inconsistency of religious discrimination with the natural-rights doctrines of freedom and equality came to be increasingly felt by thoughtful persons, though the first state constitutions still showed the persistence of older ways of thinking. More important, however, were the exigencies of the war itself. In the struggle for independence against a powerful enemy, the coöperation

[13] Quoted in Humphrey, *Nationalism and Religion*, 80.

of the so-called "popular churches" was essential; so chaplaincies went to dissenting sects in military units where such appointments would be congenial. Petitions for relief from compulsory tithes, particularly in Virginia, were more sympathetically received. Especially striking was the gradually changing attitude toward the Catholics.

Congress began to consider the possibility of Canadian coöperation and the need of a due regard for the sensibilities of French Catholics, as well as of members of the same communion in the insurgent colonies. Even in 1774, while exploiting anti-Catholic feeling on both sides of the Atlantic, Congress assumed a different tone in its "Letter to the Inhabitants of Quebec," which referred to the successful association of Protestant and Catholic cantons in the Swiss Confederation.[14] By 1775, Congress was planning an expedition to Canada, and Washington was warning the army at Cambridge against the observance of "Pope's Day," the New England commemoration of the Gunpowder Plot. The following winter Charles Carroll, the most distinguished layman among the Maryland Catholics, was associated with the free-thinking Franklin in a Congressional committee to confer with the Canadian Catholics. The committee took with them as an ecclesiastical expert Father John Carroll, the future Bishop of Baltimore. Though the mission failed in its immediate object, it was a significant episode in American church history. Then came the French alliance and a certain amount of coöperation, without a formal alliance, with the Spaniards. Catholic chaplains served the needs of the allied diplomats and soldiers. On special occasions members of Congress attended with more or less equanimity the services of the Catholic Church. There were Catholics in the Continental army itself. In some quarters there were misgivings about the effect of American associations with foreign Papists and Loyalist writers made the most of them; but on

[14] *Journals of the Continental Congress*, I, 112.

the whole there was a distinct lessening of old animosities.[15]

Both the progress of religious liberty and its limitations during this period are reflected in the first state constitutions, beginning with that of Virginia in 1776. So far as the general theory of religious liberty is concerned, the most liberal statement is to be found in the Virginia Declaration of Rights, adopted a few days before the Continental Declaration of Independence. In its earlier form, the article on religion promised "the fullest toleration in the exercise of religion." As finally adopted, the original language, with its unfortunate implications, was replaced on the initiative of James Madison by a more generous phrasing. The amended section is one of the finest documents in American history, going far beyond the philosophy of the English Act of Toleration and that of many, perhaps most, Americans even in 1776. It reads: "That religion or the duty which we owe to our Creator, and the manner of discharging it, can be directed only by reason and conviction, not by force or violence; and therefore all men are equally entitled to the free exercise of religion, according to the dictates of conscience; and that it is the mutual duty of all to practice Christian forbearance, love, and charity toward each other." It should be added that the constitution which followed the Declaration of Rights, though it made no reference to legislation applying this principle, at any rate contained nothing inconsistent with it. So much cannot be said for other constitutions of this period, as may be seen from a few typical examples.[16]

[15] Sister M. Augustina (Ray), *American Opinion of Roman Catholicism*, chap. VIII; Burnett, *Letters of Members of the Continental Congress*, IV, 297 and note 2; V, 131; James Thacher, *Military Journal* (ed. 1854), 305.

[16] Article 16 of Bill of Rights. Text in Hening, *Statutes*, IX, 110; G. Hunt, "James Madison and Religious Liberty," in American Historical Association, *Annual Report*, *1901*, I, 165–167. Madison's original proposal would have gone still further.

The Pennsylvania constitution, which included a Declaration of Rights similar to that of Virginia, also asserted the "unalienable right" of all men to worship God "according to the dictates of their own consciences and understanding." Compulsory attendance on public worship and compulsory payments for its support were condemned. No man who acknowledged "the being of a God" should suffer any abridgment of civil rights because of his religious beliefs or practice. Notwithstanding these phrases, the constitution itself did establish a religious test for membership in the Assembly; this required a declaration of belief in the divine inspiration of the Old and New Testaments.[17] In effect, Catholic disabilities were removed, but those of Jews and other non-Christians remained.

In the New York constitution, the phrasing of the clause on religion finally adopted, in spite of objections by John Jay, guaranteed the free exercise of "religious profession and worship . . . without discrimination or preference," provided that such liberty should not be held "to excuse acts of licentiousness or justify practices inconsistent with the peace or safety of this State." The phraseology advocated by Jay would have withheld complete equality from Catholics; there was such discrimination in the section on naturalization, as adopted, requiring all candidates for citizenship to "renounce all allegiance and subjection to all and every foreign king, prince, potentate, and State, in all matters ecclesiastical as well as civil." [18] As in the case of Locke, Jay's argument for discrimination was primarily political. One feature of this document was the suggestion of anticlerical feeling in the exclusion of clergymen from office, on the ground that they should devote

[17] Constitution of 1776, chap. I, article II, and its "Frame of Government," par. 10.

[18] Constitution, articles XXXVIII, XXXIX, XLII, in *The American Revolution in New York* (Albany, 1926), 337–339.

themselves to the care of souls. There was also, in the preamble of the section on religion, a reference to the danger from "spiritual oppression and intolerance wherewith the bigotry and ambition of weak and wicked priests," as well as princes, had "scourged mankind."

In the matter of church and state relations, the Massachusetts constitution of 1780 departed from colonial practice in one important respect; Catholic worship penalized under provincial law was now protected against such persecution, and regular services of this church were presently begun in Boston, where a few years earlier the service of the mass was forbidden by law. Otherwise the preferred status of the Congregational churches was continued. The legislature was to require local provision for "Protestant teachers of piety, religion, and morality," and the old plan of public taxation for the support of such teaching was retained. In substance, this meant, as in colonial times, that in most parishes there was a virtual establishment of the Congregational churches, with concessions to dissenters who could show that they were supporting the religious services of their respective denominations. This in spite of another clause solemnly declaring that "no subordination of any one sect or denomination to another" should "ever be established by law." Furthermore, state officers and members of the legislature were required to swear, or affirm, their belief in the Christian religion. Finally, no one was permitted to assume any office under the government until he had solemnly declared "that no foreign Prince, Person, Prelate, State or Potentate" had any authority, "civil, *ecclesiastical* or *spiritual*," within the Commonwealth. This test of course disqualified any conscientious Catholic.[19]

[19] Massachusetts constitution of 1780 in *Manual for the Constitutional Convention, 1917* (Boston, 1917), with annotations. See especially the "Declaration of Rights," articles II, III; "Frame of Government," chap. II, sec. 1, and chap. VI. The italics are mine.

It would be impracticable and tedious to rehearse here the corresponding provisions in other state constitutions; the general effect of the new arrangements, so far as religion was concerned, may be summed up in a few sentences. Religious liberty in the strict sense was secured; that is to say, there was henceforth freedom for diversities of religious belief and public worship. That in itself was a great advance from the days when Catholics were denied this privilege in most of the colonies. On the other hand, religious *equality* was not generally secured. Most of the states had religious tests for the holding of public office. In New Hampshire, New Jersey, and North Carolina, as well as Massachusetts, officeholders were required to be Protestants, and in South Carolina this was expected of the governor, as well as of the legislature; Delaware, like Pennsylvania, required that they should be Christians.

Church establishments and official support of churches did not at once disappear; in all of the original New England states, except, of course, Rhode Island, the standing order remained. The preferred status of the Anglican Church came to an end in Maryland, the Carolinas, and Georgia; in Virginia, the establishment practically lapsed during the war, though the process was not completed until after the peace. Meantime, Maryland and South Carolina, while depriving the Anglican Church of its exclusive privileges, both definitely recognized Christianity in their constitutions; Maryland permitted legislation for "the support of the Christian religion," leaving with the individual taxpayer the right to designate the particular denomination to which the money should go; or, if he so desired, his tax might be used for poor relief. Again, the South Carolina constitution of 1778 formally declared that the "Christian Protestant religion" should be "the established religion of this State." This was followed by most elaborate provisions regulating religious societies, which in order to receive corporate privileges had *to recognize Christianity* as "the true religion."

In short, the makers of the Revolutionary constitutions, while promising religious liberty, did not expect the state to be wholly neutral in matters of religion, and they usually took for granted a consensus of opinion in support either of Protestantism or of some form of Christianity. At the same time, a certain amount of anticlerical feeling was shown in several states by the constitutional exclusion of ministers from public office. Jefferson's later comment on this form of discrimination is of some interest. He then declared that "after 17 years more of experience and reflection" he did not approve of the disqualification of the clergy from election to public office. They had previously been "a very formidable engine against the civil and religious rights of man." They still were so, he thought, in some of these United States, but in Virginia they now seemed to claim no special privileges and should therefore have the same rights as members of other professions.[20]

The attitude of the Confederation toward religion should also be mentioned. The position of the Continental Congress in the years preceding the adoption of the articles, that is to say, during the greater part of the war period, may be described as one of sympathy with religion in general and the Christian religion in particular. At the same time, every effort was made to conciliate the various religious groups. Congress itself had its Anglican and Presbyterian chaplains. Army chaplains of various denominations were also provided for companies, regiments, and brigades, whose duties were not, however, exclusively religious. On the theory, no doubt, that cleanliness was next to godliness, they were expected to impress upon the soldiers the importance of proper sanitation, as well as to discourage profanity and vice, regarding which Congress was at times much disturbed. In this matter of civilian and mili-

[20] *Writings* (Federal ed.), IX, 143.

tary chaplaincies a practice was thus inaugurated which has come down to the present time. Congress also displayed an interest in Indian missions, largely, no doubt, with a view to strengthening American influence among the border tribes as against British and Tory efforts to secure their support.[21]

Under the Confederation there was a similar disposition to encourage religion without special reference to any particular denomination. One of the last acts of Congress before the adoption of the present constitution was the famous Northwest Ordinance, which contained two clauses dealing with religion. The first declared that "No person demeaning himself in a peaceable and orderly manner" should ever "be molested on account of his mode of worship or religious sentiments." Another article declared that religion, as well as morality and knowledge, was "necessary to good government and the happiness of mankind," and constituted one reason for the encouragement of education.[22] Generally speaking, however, Congress regarded religion as a matter reserved to the states, and in reply to a query from the Papal Nuncio in Paris regarding its attitude toward the designation of a bishop, or other director, of the Catholic clergy in the United States, it disclaimed any authority to give or refuse consent, "these powers being reserved to the states individually." [23] We may compare with this the statement made a few years earlier by John Adams: "I am for the most liberal toleration of all denominations of religionists, but I hope that Congress will never meddle with religion further than to say their own prayers, and to fast and to give thanks once a year. Let every colony have its own religion without molestation." [24]

[21] Burnett, *Letters of Members of the Continental Congress*, II, 376; E. F. Humphrey, *Nationalism and Religion*, chap. XIV.

[22] Articles I and III of the "compact."

[23] Humphrey, *Nationalism and Religion*, 430–432.

[24] *Works*, IX, 402.

So matters stood when the Federal Convention assembled at Philadelphia in 1787. No one there seems to have considered that Congress had, or should have, anything to do with religion in the states. The membership of the Convention included representatives of several Christian denominations including Catholics, as well as others who were, like Franklin, deists or freethinkers. There was little difficulty then in agreeing upon the one clause in the original constitution that deals with religion; namely, the prohibition of religious tests for federal offices.[25] This clause was of course binding only upon the federal government. There was nothing in it to interfere with such tests as then existed in the states or might thereafter be established. There was not, however, complete unanimity on this question of religious tests, when the Constitution was submitted for ratification by the states. A few persons thought some kind of test desirable; others held that there should have been some more definite guarantee of religious liberty.[26] In response to the latter demand, the first amendment to the Constitution provided that "Congress shall make no law respecting an establishment of religion, or prohibiting the free exercise thereof." This provision, like the prohibition of religious tests, had of course no effect on the legislation of the states. No doubt, however, such a declaration had a certain moral effect. In any case, Congressional intervention in these matters was obviously out of the question.[27]

[25] Article VI, par. 3.

[26] See e.g. Martin's statement in M. Farrand, *The Records of the Federal Convention of 1787* (New Haven, 1911), III, 227; and for other illustrations, Humphrey, *Nationalism and Religion*, 462–479.

[27] It is worth noting here that there was a definite interrelation between independence and union in the political sphere and certain organic changes in the churches. As a result of the Revolution, the Anglican churches of the colonies found it necessary to terminate their organic relations with the Church of England, which was closely associated with the British monarchy, though the new "Protestant Episcopal" dioceses remained in spiritual com-

What has been called the American tradition of the separation of church and state was, therefore, far from being universally accepted at the close of the Revolutionary War. That result, with certain qualifications to be considered later, was the outcome of another half century of experience and public discussion. In this further advance the honor of leadership belongs to Virginia.

There were various factors favorable to early action in the Old Dominion. The association of the Anglican establishment with the provincial regime was now, in the new republican order, an embarrassment rather than an advantage. Though many of the clergy adhered to the American cause, some of the most conspicuous had taken the Loyalist side and left the state. The years immediately preceding the war had also been

munion with the English church. The Dutch, and German, Reformed Churches now became fully independent of the ecclesiastical authorities in Holland. Again, the Methodists, with Wesley's approval, became a distinct denomination in this country, even before their English leader had definitely separated from the Church of England. Finally, the American Catholics, though of course maintaining their allegiance to the Roman Papacy, were detached from the jurisdiction of the English Vicar Apostolic. The movement toward unity illustrates a similar parallelism between state and church developments, notably in the case of the Catholics, the Episcopalians, the Methodists, and the Presbyterians. The American Catholics were brought together under the direction of a new American bishop. Independent dioceses of the Episcopal Church were organized in a bicameral "General Convention," analogous to the Federal Congress, with bishops in one house acting with elected diocesan representatives—lay as well as clerical —in the other. A little earlier the Methodists adopted a constitution for the country at large, with bishops (at first called superintendents) and a representative "General Conference." Certain other Protestant bodies were too insistent on the independence of their local congregations to take a similar course, but the Presbyterians who had taken steps toward union before the Revolution now formed for the first time an organization for all the former colonies with a "General Assembly" of representatives chosen by the clergy and laity.

marked by a serious rift between the clergy and influential members of the laity on the question of ministerial stipends. "The Parson's Cause," in which Patrick Henry opposed the claims of the clergy, illustrates the association of the church question with the issue of local self-government, as against the royal disallowance of a provincial statute opposed by the established clergy. Not less important was the rapid growth, largely owing to the Great Awakening whose effects were felt longer here than in New England, of the so-called "popular" denominations, more particularly the New Side Presbyterians and the Baptists. Finally, among the political leaders there was a considerable group who, though more or less definitely affiliated with Anglican parishes, had come under the influence of eighteenth-century deism, or through personal contacts outside the church had come to sympathize with the grievances of the dissenters. Of the first group was Thomas Jefferson, whose thinking was strongly tinged with anticlericalism. Representatives of the latter group were Patrick Henry and, more significantly in the later phases of the discussion, James Madison. At Princeton, Madison had come under the influence of its Scotch Presbyterian President, John Witherspoon, one of the most aggressive opponents of church establishments.

After the adoption of the state constitution, Jefferson became an active member of a legislative committee on religion to which were referred the complaints of the dissenting churches.[28] The outcome was the gradual breakdown of the establishment, though in the face of a considerable opposition. Dissenters were exempted from the payment of tithes; the law providing for the collection of ministerial salaries was first suspended and then repealed; dissenting ministers were authorized to celebrate marriages; and acts for the suppression of heresy were repealed. Before the war ended, the estab-

[28] Virginia House of Delegates, *Journal*, 1776, pp. 7–63 *passim* (October and November entries).

lishment had lost most of its special privileges and also suffered seriously in prestige.[29]

Presently the discussion entered a new phase. A considerable number of responsible leaders, including some Presbyterians and such relatively liberal churchmen as Patrick Henry, were seriously disturbed by the apparent decline of religion and morality, resulting in part from abnormal wartime conditions and partly, they believed, from the diffusion of deistic ideas. In the opinion of this group, there could no longer be any question of special privileges for a particular religious denomination, but they feared the consequences of an abrupt change from the old method of compulsory church rates to purely voluntary contributions.[30] Their point of view was represented in the so-called "General Assessment" plan for the support of religion, according to which the taxpayer might elect to have his money go either to the denomination of his choice or to education. To this proposal, however, most of the dissenters already accustomed to voluntary support were strongly opposed. Jefferson was then abroad and the chief antagonist of the bill was Madison, who argued that religion was a subject beyond the competence of the civil government; also that it would gain rather than lose by detachment from the state. This opposition defeated the "Assessment" bill and finally in 1785 both houses of the state legislature passed an Act for establishing Religious Freedom, which had been drafted by Jefferson.[31]

The long preamble of this famous document began "Whereas Almighty God hath created the mind free," and

[29] Lingley, *Transition in Virginia*, 198–203; Eckenrode, *Separation of Church and State in Virginia*, chap. IV.

[30] W. W. Henry, *Patrick Henry, Life, Correspondence and Speeches*, II (New York, 1891), chap. XXXI.

[31] Details, with documents, are in Eckenrode, *Separation of Church and State in Virginia*, chaps. V–VII.

after reciting the arguments for separation on theoretical and practical grounds proceeded to a brief enacting clause. This substantially accomplished the separation of church and state, excluding any form of compulsion, whether in the form of public taxation in support of the church or through requiring attendance on any kind of religious service. Furthermore, the rights guaranteed by this statute were asserted to be "of the natural rights of mankind." Repeal of the law by any subsequent legislature, even though technically within its power, would be "an infringement of natural right." [32] It is well known that the authorship of this bill was regarded by Jefferson as so important that he included it in the epitaph which he prepared for his tomb at Monticello, as one of his three principal contributions, the other two being the Declaration of Independence and the founding of the University of Virginia.

In New England, separation came much less easily and only after a controversy extending over half a century. In Connecticut the issue was substantially determined in 1818 when that state, for the first time, adopted a constitution to replace its seventeenth-century charter. This constitution not only guaranteed liberty of religious profession and worship, but also promised that no person should be legally obliged to support any church, except that of his own choice, and that no Christian denomination or mode of worship should receive any legal preference.[33] In Massachusetts, the process of separation was completed by the adoption of a constitutional amendment in 1833. In general, the forces at work for and against separation in these two states and in New Hampshire were similar. For our present purposes it will be sufficient if we follow the development in Massachusetts.

[32] Text in Hening, *Statutes of Virginia*, XII, 84–86.

[33] Constitution of 1818, Article I, secs. 3 and 4, and Article VII, secs. 1 and 2. For accounts of the movement toward separation, see Greene, *Religious Liberty in Connecticut*, and Purcell, *Connecticut in Transition*.

We may take as our starting point the constitutional provisions of 1780. In brief, these were, as we have seen, general declarations for religious liberty and against the subordination of one sect to another, strangely combined, however, with the requirement of public support for Protestant teachers of religion and morality. This meant in practice an establishment of the Congregational churches in most of the towns, mitigated somewhat by the provision that the taxes of certain dissenters might be applied to the support of the ministers whose services they attended. The whole theory of taxation for religious purposes was especially objectionable to Quakers and Baptists, quite apart from any practical hardship involved. During the next half century, the Baptists were the most vigorous and effective champions of religious equality. Even within the standing order, there were many who disapproved of religious tests for public office.[34] A notable example is that of Joseph Hawley, the outstanding leader of the Connecticut Valley Whigs in the Revolution. Himself a deacon in the Northampton church of which Jonathan Edwards had been the pastor, he attacked the test oath in language which might well be pondered by advocates of test oaths at the present time. "Did our Father Confessors," he asked "imagine that a man who had not so much fear of God in his heart, as to restrain him from acting dishonestly and knavishly in the trust of a Senator or representative, would hesitate a moment to subscribe that declaration?" Hawley was chosen a member of the first state senate, declined to take the oath, explaining that, though he had been "a professed Christian nearly 40 years," he was debarred from taking his seat in the legislature "by the unconscionable not to say dishonorable terms" of the constitution.[35]

In the next three decades legislation within the general scope of the religious clauses of the constitution modified de-

[34] Meyer, *Church and State in Massachusetts*, chap. IV.

[35] Quoted in E. F. Brown, *Joseph Hawley* (New York, Columbia University Press, 1931), 182–183.

tails of the system, as, for instance, by exempting Quakers from church taxes altogether. There were court decisions interpreting issues raised from time to time by dissenters. During most of this period the defense of the established order, in Massachusetts as well as in Connecticut, was closely associated with Federalist conservatism in politics, while the Jeffersonian Republican party, which drew much of its membership from the dissenters, was more liberal in this respect. Meantime, there were actual cases of imprisonment for failure on the part of dissenters to pay church taxes. Finally, however, in 1811 a Jeffersonian governor and legislature passed the Religious Freedom Act of 1811 which marked a distinct advance. Church taxes were still to be collected, although it was made easier under the new law for dissenters to avoid payments in support of the Congregational churches. The Federalist Chief Justice, Theophilus Parker, spoke of the deplorable tendency of the new law "to destroy all the decency and regularity of public worship," but he recognized the necessity of accepting "such acts of the legislature, as they have the constitutional authority to make." [36]

An important landmark in the history of disestablishment was the State Constitutional Convention of 1820–1821. The members of this body were a distinguished group, including ex-President John Adams, Justice Story, and young Daniel Webster, who had recently come to Massachusetts from New Hampshire. By this time, the Congregational churches were sharply divided by the theological conflict between orthodox Trinitarians and Unitarians, and this controversy had weakened the upholders of the old order. Curiously enough, the Unitarians who had broken away from the traditional theology supplied some of the most stubborn defenders of the church-state system. In this Convention of 1820, old John Adams proved to be one of the more liberal members. He

[36] Meyer, *Church and State*, 155–157.

moved unsuccessfully that the equal protection of the law promised to all Christians should be extended to include "all men of all religions." On the other hand, the rising young statesman, Daniel Webster, defended the test oath and opposed an amendment that would have ended the establishment and placed the churches upon a voluntary basis. Leverett Saltonstall of Salem attacked the proposed amendment as a "fearful experiment" and predicted that, in case of its adoption, "Our temples of worship will decay and fall around us." Furthermore, the vested rights of the established churches must be held sacred. "Let us not," he continued, "in one hour destroy the venerable work of two centuries." [37]

In the end, the Convention recommended a moderate concession not eliminating church taxes altogether but clarifying the right of all dissenters to contribute their church taxes to the support of their own pastors and putting Catholics in this respect in the same position as the Protestant denominations. It was also proposed to repeal the constitutional provision authorizing legislation to compel church attendance. Even this concession was defeated by an overwhelming majority of the voters of the state, though the eastern counties of Suffolk, Middlesex, and Barnstable voted for it. The voters approved another amendment, however, abolishing religious tests for office, on the ground that the assuming of civil office was not "a suitable occasion" for "the declaration of belief in the Christian religion." Somewhat naïve, perhaps, was the statement of the Convention "that every man who is accepted for office, in this community, must have such sentiments of religious duty as relate to his fitness for the place to which he is called." In short, the advocates of separation had made some progress but not much. [38]

Meantime the population of the Commonwealth was

[37] *Manual for the Constitutional Convention, 1917*, 30–33.
[38] *Ibid.*, 32–37.

steadily becoming more heterogeneous from the point of view of religious traditions. The older dissenting groups of Baptists and Episcopalians were increasing in numbers and influence. The growth of Methodism and Universalism since the Revolution brought to the opposition a substantial number of new voters. Finally, Irish Catholic immigration, though much less than in later years, still further reinforced the advocates of separation. As against this gathering force of dissent, the former upholders of the standing order were hopelessly divided by the hardening of the cleavage between Orthodox and Unitarian Congregationalists, which had now become two permanently separated denominations. According to the Dedham case, decided in 1820 by the State Supreme Court, the property of a local church belonged to the taxpaying parishioners as a whole, rather than to the communicant members of the church only, who were more likely to be orthodox than their noncommunicant associates. Thus the adherents of the old faith were often obliged to form new churches, which had, like the dissenters, to depend on voluntary contributions, and therefore lost interest in the maintenance of the old establishment.[39] In 1831, a representative journal of this party took a definite stand against church taxes: "To say that our religion cannot be supported without the aid of establishment and law," was, according to this writer, "to disgrace it in the eyes of the world, and to cast reproach on its maker." [40]

So it came about that in the year after Andrew Jackson's triumphant reëlection to the presidency of the United States the ecclesiastical conservatism of Massachusetts suffered another defeat in the adoption of Article XI of the amendments to the Constitution of 1780. This amendment placed all religious denominations on an equal footing of voluntary support,

[39] Cf. E. Buck, *Massachusetts Ecclesiastical Law* (Boston, 1866), chaps. IV and V.

[40] Quoted in Meyer, *Church and State in Massachusetts*, 218.

and, as interpreted by a subsequent decision of the State Supreme Court, effectively prevented the establishment of a state church. A striking illustration of the change in public opinion was the majority of nearly ten to one in favor of a proposal more advanced than that which had been overwhelmingly defeated by the electorate only twelve years before.[41]

[41] *Manual for the Constitutional Convention*, 1917, 38–39 and note, 177.

V

After "Separation"

WHEN in 1833 the people of Massachusetts ratified the eleventh amendment to their state constitution, they closed an important chapter in the history of American church and state relations. The process of separation, in the usual sense of that word, was substantially complete. Individual freedom of conscience, the equal right of all orderly religious groups to maintain their own forms of public worship, prohibition of public taxation for the support of any particular church—these principles were now written into the constitutional law of the American commonwealths. Fairly typical of the state constitutions in force during the first half of the nineteenth century is the following declaration in the Illinois constitution of 1818: "That all men have a natural and indefeasible right to worship Almighty God according to the dictates of their own consciences; that no man can of right be compelled to attend, erect, or support any place of worship, or to maintain any ministry against his consent; that no human authority can in any case whatever, control or interfere with the rights of conscience; and that no preference shall ever be given by law to any religious establishments or modes of worship." [1]

Religious tests for public office were gradually abandoned, but a few survived down to the period of the Civil War and some even later—chiefly south of the Mason-Dixon line. [2]

---

[1] Article VIII, sec. 3.

[2] These constitutional provisions conveniently assembled in C. H. Moehlman, comp., *American Constitutions and Religion* (Berne, Indiana, 1938).

Pennsylvania, whose first state constitution limited membership in the legislature to Christians, carried over into its nineteenth-century constitutions a clause that qualified the exclusion of religious tests by limiting this guarantee to persons who acknowledged the being of God and a future state of rewards and punishments. Other states that retained similar qualifications were Maryland, North Carolina, Tennessee, Mississippi, and Arkansas. North Carolina excluded from office any one who denied the truth of the Christian religion, and Maryland had a similar provision, with a special concession to Jews who might qualify by a declaration of belief in a future state of rewards and punishments. On the closely related matter of court tests for jurors and witnesses, there was no uniform action during the nineteenth century. In several states atheists were disqualified by constitutional provisions, statutes, or the application of common-law principles. Thus the Arkansas constitution of 1836 declared that no atheist should be "allowed his oath in any court." Tocqueville noted a New York case in which testimony was rejected on this ground;[3] in recent years the issue has again been raised, notably in New Jersey and North Carolina. On the other hand, many state constitutions have expressly forbidden such tests: such action by New York and Iowa in 1846 was followed in the next half century by several Western states. The Oregon constitution of 1859 not only prohibited religious tests for jurors and witnesses, but forbade the questioning of a witness as to his religious belief in a way "to affect the weight of his testimony."

One method of separating church and state that occurred frequently in the eighteenth- and early nineteenth-century constitutions was the disqualification of clergymen from important public posts. Though New York was one of the first to

[3] See his *Democracy in America* (Bowen's revision of Reeve's translation; Cambridge, Mass., 1862), I, 391, with editor's note.

take such action, she was exceptional in this respect among the Northern states, and omitted this provision in the constitution of 1821. In the South, however, this disqualification of the clergy was fairly common, both on the seaboard and among the new commonwealths of the Southwest, including Delaware, the Carolinas, Georgia, Kentucky, Tennessee, Mississippi, Louisiana, Missouri, and Texas. No such provisions occur in the Northwestern states. Of special interest is the case of Wisconsin where a clerical disqualification clause was proposed in the constitutional convention of 1847, but was reported adversely as an unfair discrimination against a particular profession.[4]

Though American theory and practice are against any organic connection between the state and any particular church, this has not prevented recognition by state and federal governments of religion *per se* as a desirable part of the social order, as, for instance, by religious phraseology in many of the state constitutions. From the era of the Revolution to the present time, religious exercises have frequently formed a part of official ceremonies. Congress and state legislatures have their chaplains, paid from public funds; provision is also made for the service of priests or ministers in the Army, the Navy, and in penal and charitable institutions, due regard being had to the distribution of such appointments among the various denominations in proportion to their numerical strength in the country at large and in the particular groups to be served. In the Army, for instance, the office of the Chief of Chaplains reported, in June 1941, one hundred and thirty-six army chaplains chosen from twenty religious denominations. There were also more than twelve hundred reserve chaplains representing over thirty denominations, including Catholics, Protestants, and Jews. At that time the regular Navy had more than a hun-

[4] Zollmann, *American Church Law*, 430–431; *Journal of the Convention* (Madison, 1847), 85, 208.

dred of these officers, besides more than fifty in the Naval Reserve.[5]

The most substantial contribution made by the state to the maintenance of religious institutions is undoubtedly the exemption of their property from public taxation—a principle accepted throughout the country, though with qualifications that vary in detail from one state to another. In general, the exemption does not cover all property owned by a church, but only what is actually used "for religious purposes." Such exemption of church property began at a time when direct financial support of religion was regarded as legitimate. Since the principle of separation has been accepted, exemption is justified on the ground of social services—cultural, philanthropic, and ethical—incident to the distinctly religious work of the churches.[6] It is obviously impossible to deal with the large number of judicial decisions interpreting the precise degree and kind of use that will justify exemption. Two things, however, may be said about the present situation: first, there has been a great increase in the extent and value of such exempt holdings; and, second, the question has been seriously raised, though as yet by comparatively small minorities, whether such a contribution to religious institutions, even in this indirect form, is quite consistent with the doctrine of "separation."

Another form of state aid to religion which has continued since formal separation is the restraint by penal law of language regarded as blasphemous and therefore offensive to religious-minded persons, with possible disturbance of the public peace. A notable instance of prosecution for blasphemy

[5] Letters from the office of the Chief of Chaplains, United States Army, June 4, 12, 1941, and from the Head of Chaplains Division, United States Navy, June 13, 1941.

[6] Zollman, *American Civil Church Law* (Columbia University Studies in History, Economics, and Public Law), chap. IX (chap. X in his *American Church Law*, 1933).

occurred in Massachusetts in the eighteen thirties, when the freethinker, Abner Kneeland, was indicted, tried, convicted, and imprisoned for publishing "a certain scandalous, impious, obscene, blasphemous and profane libel of and concerning God." The doubtful advantage from any point of view, of such prosecution is suggested by the petition for Kneeland's pardon signed by several clergymen, not only by such liberals as Channing, Parker, and Emerson, but by leading Baptist ministers [7] who were quite out of sympathy with Kneeland's views. Much of this blasphemy legislation represents a survival from earlier periods, but prosecutions occur from time to time and the general principle implied has been maintained by the courts of several states.[8] Now, as in Kneeland's time, there are clergymen who do not feel the need of such protection for religion. A few years ago three clergymen appeared before a committee of the Massachusetts legislature to urge repeal of the blasphemy law then in force in that state.[9]

If the state still gives a measure of support to religion, it also qualifies its guarantee of religious liberty in the interest of public order. The New York constitution, for example, has always contained a clause providing that liberty of conscience "shall not be so construed as to excuse acts of licentiousness or justify practices inconsistent with the peace or safety of this state." [10] Obviously such a reservation allows some latitude in interpretation by legislatures and courts and may be abused, but it is hard to see how such discretion can be avoided. The most striking example of the application of this principle is the action of the federal government in relation to the Mormon

[7] W. H. Allison, "Abner Kneeland," in *Dictionary of American Biography*, and references there cited; H. S. Commager, "The Blasphemy of Abner Kneeland," in *New England Quarterly*, VIII, 29–41.

[8] Zollmann, *American Church Law*, 39–41.

[9] *The New York Times*, January 29, 1930.

[10] Constitution of 1777, Article XXXVIII.

teaching and practice of polygamy. The controversy arising on this issue was active for half a century until finally settled by the decision of the Mormon church to abandon this practice and the admission of Utah to the Union on that basis. The controversy has also left its mark in the constitutions of Utah, Idaho, and Oklahoma, all of which specifically prohibit plural marriages. On the other hand, the state has sometimes relaxed the ordinary rules of law out of respect for religious scruples pleaded in good faith. Familiar examples are the concessions made to members of the Society of Friends, the Moravians, and the Mennonites with respect to the taking of oaths and the bearing of arms. On this problem of reconciling the sovereignty of the state with the claims of the individual conscience, more will be said later.

At this point, we may turn for a moment to the American situation as seen by European observers about a hundred years ago. The most philosophical of our European visitors in the era of Jacksonian democracy was doubtless Alexis de Tocqueville, who came to the United States during Jackson's administration. His testimony is of peculiar interest because it was recorded at a time when the American tradition seemed to have been definitely set. Having left Europe with a keen sense of the new problems created by the rise of democracy and the attitude of its advocates toward religion, he looked to the United States as a kind of social laboratory. The experiments tried there should, he thought, be instructive for the scholars and statesmen of the old world. What had religion to hope, or fear, from democracy? In his *Democracy in America,* first published in 1835, Tocqueville recalled the theory of the eighteenth-century *philosophes* that religious zeal would fade as liberty advanced and enlightenment prevailed. On the contrary, it seemed to him that in America religion and liberty, or democracy, were intimately associated. In his opinion, this was true not only of Protestants but also of Catholics, though the

European members of that communion feared, with some reason, the anti-Christian temper of many democratic leaders. What was the explanation of this difference between America and Europe? Tocqueville found it in the separation of church and state and in the general abstention of the clergy from politics. He noted in this connection the constitutional provisions already mentioned which in certain states barred clergymen from public office. He believed, however, that in any case they were disposed to avoid party activities. Thus they escaped the disastrous consequences, so evident in Europe under the system of church establishment, of allowing religion to become entangled with transient issues and institutions. It seemed to him that the American people were, in spite of the multiplicity of sects among them, agreed in thinking religion, and especially Christian morality, essential to the maintenance of a democracy.[11]

Hardly less interesting than Tocqueville's comments are those of the distinguished English writer, Harriet Martineau, in her *Society in America*. During her two years' stay in the United States, she traveled widely and met a remarkable number of representative people in various walks of life, from President Jackson down. Miss Martineau thoroughly approved the "voluntary system," as she called it, as contrasted with the ecclesiastical establishments of Europe. "America," she wrote, "has left it to the Old World to fortify Christianity by establishments, and has triumphantly shown that a great nation may be trusted to its religious instincts to provide for its religious wants." [12] Referring especially to the recently adopted Massachusetts amendment of 1833, she believed that the result fully justified the confidence of those who had

[11] A. de Tocqueville, *Démocratie en Amérique* (ed. 1864), I, 18; II, 208–211, 221–232.

[12] Martineau, *Society in America* (London, 1837), II, Part IV, pp. 335 ff.

"faith enough in Christianity to see that it needs no protection from the state, but will commend itself to human hearts better without." [13] As an advanced liberal, however, Miss Martineau believed that social pressure was still a real obstacle to full religious freedom. She noted, for instance, that "a religious young Christian legislator" in Boston had been denounced in conservative circles for his efforts to secure the repeal of a Massachusetts law disqualifying atheists as witnesses in the courts. She commented also on the prevalence of sectarian feeling, particularly as directed against the Catholics, and referred to the disgraceful mob attack on the Ursuline Convent near Boston, which took place a few weeks before her arrival in this country. [14]

Measured by constitutions and laws, toleration and religious equality had made remarkable gains since the close of the colonial era. It was yet to be seen how far the ground thus gained would be maintained in a changing and increasingly heterogeneous society. In the century which has passed since Tocqueville and Martineau set down their impressions, the problem of mutual adjustment among social groups, with varying and often mutually antagonistic religious traditions, has become far more complex. Some issues which excited intense feeling a hundred years ago have lost their interest; others of a more fundamental sort are still with us.

In the native-born population of the early eighteen thirties —largely descendants of the old colonial stocks from the British Isles and from Germany—a Protestant outlook on religion could, by and large, be taken for granted. There were, of course, some professed freethinkers, a few Jews, and a considerably larger number of Catholics. Generally speaking,

[13] *Ibid.*, 349.

[14] *Ibid.*, 316–324. Compare with these foreign comments Robert Baird's *Religion in America* (New York, 1844) and James Bryce's *American Commonwealth*, II (any edition).

these groups were not then strongly represented among the influential classes. Miss Martineau observed that even among religiously indifferent persons there were few who did not "carefully profess Christianity in one form or another"; so far as the influential groups were concerned, there were probably few who did not favor some form of Protestant Christianity, even though they might not be actual members of any church.

During the next quarter century the situation was radically changed. There was a great wave of Irish immigration, now mainly Catholic instead of largely Protestant as in colonial days, and another not less important from Germany. The German immigrants, though still predominantly non-Catholic, included many members of that communion, besides a considerable number of freethinkers, especially among the leaders; the latter and many of the orthodox German Protestants reacted strongly against the Puritan tradition, as, for instance, in such matters as Sunday observance. In the South these newcomers were comparatively few; it was on the northern seaboard and in the Middle West that their influence was most felt. Irish and Germans were numerous in both areas; the former were relatively important in the Eastern cities while the German influence was especially significant in the "Old Northwest." In the latter half of the nineteenth century, the Scandinavian immigrants, mainly Protestant, came in increasing numbers. Finally, at the turn of the century and in the years immediately preceding and following the World War of 1914, came other European stocks, Catholic and Jewish, for whom the problem of adjustment to the older American tradition was still more difficult—difficult for them and difficult also for people of the older stock. It is not necessary to elaborate these familiar facts in the history of American immigration; yet they form an essential background for our story of religion in its relation to politics.

Especially in communities, East or West, where the descendants of the Puritans and the inheritors of their ideas had largely determined social policies, the native population found itself more and more confronted first by strong minorities of newcomers who "knew not Pharaoh," and then gradually in many cases by actual majorities of aliens. Difficulties arose not always on strictly religious issues but often in the borderland of social conventions rooted in, or associated with, religious traditions. Ideas of education and ethical training which might be adjusted among different kinds of Protestants were harder to deal with when between Catholics and Protestants, or between Christians on one side and Jews or thoroughgoing secularists on the other.

Before discussing specific problems of church and state in the nineteenth and twentieth centuries—a discussion which must in any case be very brief—let us consider a fundamental issue that underlies the opposing positions now taken on some very practical questions. The problem, roughly stated, is this: Assuming that the church, or churches, on the one side and the state on the other have their appropriate spheres of action, are they mutually independent within those spheres? Does the church, for instance, possess inherent rights, independently derived and therefore not to be abridged or controlled by the state? Or is the corporate action of the church, in external matters at least, subject like that of other nonpolitical associations to the control of the sovereign state? Extreme positions on this issue entered largely into the ecclesiastico-political conflicts of medieval and modern Europe and are not wholly obsolete even here.

The Catholic position was authoritatively stated in the encyclical letter of Pope Leo XIII, *De Immortale Dei*, "On the Christian Constitution of States," issued in 1885.[15] In this

[15] English translation in Ryan and Millar, *The State and the Church*, 1–25, especially 7, 14, 18.

he restated the traditional principle of the two spheres: "The Almighty, therefore, has appointed the charge of the human race between two powers, the ecclesiastical and the civil, the one being set over divine, the other over human things. Each in its kind is supreme, each has fixed limits within which it is contained . . . there is, we may say, an orbit traced out within which the action of each is brought into play by its own native right." The Pope rejected emphatically the absolutist theory of the state which regarded the church as not different from other societies in the state, possessing like them "no right nor any legal power of action, save that which she holds by the favor and concession of the government." On the contrary, he insisted, the church was "no less than the State itself . . . a society perfect in its own nature and its own right." It is a far cry from the Pope to Mr. Harold Laski, but it is interesting to note that Father Ryan in his commentary on this encyclical of Pope Leo XIII quotes with approval Laski's protest against the Austinian theory of sovereignty.[16] The position of the church has certainly something in common with that of those modern students of political theory who have reacted strongly against absolutist conceptions of the state, in the interest not only of the church, but of other societies in the commonwealth.

In his suggestive little book on *Churches in the Modern State*, the late Dr. Figgis conveniently summarized the absolutist view of the relation of the state to other forms of association. "In this view," he wrote, "apart from the State, the real society—and from individuals, the living members of the State—there are no active social unities; all other apparent communal unities are directly or indirectly delegations either of State powers or of individuals."[17] A similar idea was expressed more bluntly by the French statesman, Émile Combes, who led the separationists in France during the early years of

[16] *Ibid.*, 41, 43.

[17] London and New York, Longmans, Green and Company, Inc., pp. 175–177.

the present century: "There are," he declared, "there can be, no rights except the right of the State, and there are, and there can be no other authority than the authority of the Republic." [18] A recent American statement is that of the late Charles C. Marshall in his book, *The Roman Catholic Church in the Modern State*. Referring specifically to "the right of propaganda and the right to acquire property within the State," he says: "These rights which the Church of Rome claims as inherent, other associative bodies or corporations, religious as well as secular, acknowledge to be created by and received from the State." [19]

Statements of theory like those just quoted may perhaps seem academic rather than practical. Yet such ideas, more or less consciously held, will probably affect the mental attitudes of many persons as they approach certain very practical issues of the present and future. For the present, however, let us consider some of the actual contacts between church and state that remain, in spite of their so-called separation. In this connection an analogy drawn from our political history may be suggestive. In 1861, when Abraham Lincoln was confronted with the secession of the Southern states and the formation of the new Confederacy, he pointed out that political separation, even if successfully maintained, would still leave difficult problems of mutual adjustment. "Physically speaking," he said, "we cannot separate. We cannot remove our respective sections from each other nor build an impassable wall between them." [20] Though the analogy is not perfect, something like this might be said of the relations of church and state in this or any country, after their formal separation. There still remain difficult boundary questions, conflicting interests, and traditional antagonisms.

[18] Quoted, *ibid.*, 56.
[19] P. 211.
[20] First Inaugural Address.

Whatever may be thought of the inherent and spiritual rights of the church, or churches, in the modern state, they require for the protection of their material interests the advantages to be secured through legal recognition by the state of their corporate status or of some approximation to that status in the form of trusteeship. In most of the American commonwealths the law definitely provides for the formal incorporation of ecclesiastical societies. Exceptional cases, due to historical circumstances, are those of Virginia and West Virginia, the latter state having taken over the traditional policy of the Old Dominion, of which it was originally a part. There the struggle for emancipation from the Anglican establishment left behind a persistent distrust of ecclesiastical corporations. In the heat of that controversy, an act was passed for the incorporation of the Episcopal clergy and vestries, but it was soon repealed. The ultimate result was a clause in the nineteenth-century constitution of Virginia, which is still in force, forbidding the legislature to incorporate "any church or religious denomination," but authorizing it "to secure the title to church property to an extent to be limited by law." [21] The West Virginia constitution contains substantially the same provision;[22] that of Missouri does not go so far but Article III, section 8, of its present constitution provides: "That no religious corporation can be established in this State, except such as may be created under a general law for the purpose only of holding title to such real estate as may be prescribed by law for church edifices, parsonages, and cemeteries." [23] The forms of incorporation for churches vary from one state to another and the details are not essential for our present discussion.

[21] Constitution of 1850, Article IV, sec. 32; Constitution of 1902, sec. 59.

[22] Constitution of 1861–1863, Article XI, sec. 2; Constitution of 1872, Article VI, sec. 47.

[23] Constitution of 1875, Article II, sec. 8.

The Catholic Church has had some difficulty in securing forms of incorporation adapted to its ecclesiastical constitution. Under earlier state laws, trusteeships were created through which it was possible for lay trustees to control parish affairs in defiance of the ecclesiastical authorities and the canon law of the church. A number of serious conflicts resulted, and in 1866 the Plenary Council of the American bishops, meeting in Baltimore, complained that, while in general the state governments had been considerate, there were still several states in which the church was "not yet permitted legally to make those arrangements for the security of Church Property, which are in accordance with the canons and discipline of the Catholic Church." [24] From the Catholic point of view, the situation has been substantially improved since the Baltimore pronouncement was made. A recent student of the subject notes that occasional disputes still occur which might be simplified "if the church were allowed greater freedom in incorporation laws." The New York statute of 1911 is regarded as especially satisfactory from the point of view of this church.[25]

Other examples of state control of church temporalities are the law of eminent domain, under which ecclesiastical as well as private property may be taken for public purposes with suitable compensation, and certain restrictions on the acquisition of real estate. Such restrictions illustrate the principle of mortmain, for which the English colonists had precedents in medieval statutes. The most interesting case is that of Maryland, whose present law has a background going back to the seventeenth-century controversy in which Lord Baltimore applied the law of mortmain to Jesuit purchases of land from the Indians. The constitution of this state still requires the consent

[24] Billington, *Protestant Crusade*, 38 ff., 295 ff.; *Concilii Plenarii Baltimorensis . . . Acta et Decreta, II* (Baltimore, 1868), pp. cix-cx.

[25] P. J. Dignan, *A History of the Legal Incorporation of Church Properties in the United States* (Washington, 1933), chap. VIII, esp. p. 268.

of the legislature for every transfer of property to a church, religious order, or ecclesiastical personage as such in excess of five acres for a church building, parsonage, and burying ground.[26] Other states have limited the amount of real estate acquired by any church to a specified number of acres. A recent student of American church law has suggested that such legislation is not of much importance in the United States, since the available quantity of land is great and its speculative value comparatively small.[27] That has doubtless been true in the past, but it may not always be so.

Though the civil law does not concern itself with strictly religious issues, the decisions of courts may vitally affect the interests of churches, as in the famous Dedham case in Massachusetts, which enabled the majority of voters in a Congregational parish to retain ecclesiastical property as against an orthodox majority of the communicants. In general, the civil courts are disposed in case of property disputes to follow the decisions of the appropriate church court. In the leading case of *Watson v. Jones* resulting from a conflict among the Kentucky Presbyterians, the Supreme Court of the United States declared that whenever "questions of discipline, or of faith, or ecclesiastical rule, custom or law" had been decided by the church court of last resort, the civil courts "must accept such decisions as final, and as binding on them in their application to the case before them." [28] It should be said, however, that this decision has been criticized as too sweeping and as likely in some cases to result in serious injustice.

Of more general interest than the strictly legal aspect of church and state relations are the interactions between religion and partisan politics. Something has already been said of religious issues in the preliminaries of the Revolution, notably the

[26] Constitution of 1864, Declaration of Rights, Article 38.
[27] Zollman, *American Church Law*, 164–168.
[28] U. S. *Reports*, 679–738, esp. p. 727.

use made by the radical leaders of the proposal for an American episcopate and the concessions made to the Canadian Catholics in the Quebec Act of 1774. After the Revolution, the adoption of the new federal system, and the outbreak of the French Revolution, the more extreme Federalists sought to exploit antiforeign feeling by denouncing the Jeffersonian Republicans as allies of the French Jacobins, and much was said about French infidelity as a menace to American religious institutions. In New England, the Republicans tended to favor the disestablishment of the Congregational churches, while the Federalists generally supported the standing order in the church as well as in the state. In the words of one of Jefferson's Connecticut followers, that State was "under the management of the old firm of Moses and Aaron";[29] that is to say, the clergy were valuable allies of the conservative lawgivers. In this period of Federalist-Republican politics, the anti-Catholic element was comparatively unimportant.

It was quite another story, however, in the four decades between our so-called Era of Good Feeling and the Civil War, when the rising tide of immigration, especially from Ireland and Germany, led many men to fear that alien influences would endanger the maintenance of American institutions in state and church. Among the chief objects of attack were Irish and German Catholics and so-called "infidel" Germans. The result was a series of nativistic movements against foreign influences generally; on the religious side, special emphasis was laid on the Catholic Church and the supposed menace of the Pope as a "foreign potentate." It is not necessary to develop in detail this familiar phase of American political history which has been dealt with in a number of monographs on nativism in particular areas; the religious phase of nativism has recently been treated at length in Billington's *Protestant*

[29] Quoted in R. J. Purcell, *Connecticut in Transition, 1775–1818* (Washington, D. C., 1918), 212.

Crusade,[30] which has an extensive bibliography. Only a few high points can be noted here.

The anti-Catholic agitation of the eighteen twenties gradually spread and became more aggressive in the next three decades. In 1834 occurred the disgraceful episode of the burning of the Ursuline Convent at Charlestown, Massachusetts, by a mob recruited largely from Boston. In the thirties and forties nativism, with its anti-Catholic propaganda, became an important factor in local politics, particularly in the Eastern cities. In 1843 there was an "American Republican" party in New York City which presently had branches in other Eastern states. In 1844 the new party carried elections contests in New York City and Philadelphia; in New York especially, Catholic efforts to secure a share of the school funds had intensified religious partisanship. In the latter half of this decade, there was a temporary decline of political nativism. The anti-Catholic agitation continued and in the fifties came the formation of the "Know-Nothing" lodges and the organization of the American party; in the elections of 1854 and 1855 this party carried several states. Though in the end its presidential candidate secured the vote of only one state in the next presidential election, it was widely believed for a time that the Americans had a fair chance of winning.[31]

The national platform of the American party in 1855 devoted two of its fourteen articles to the religious issue. One of them denounced "the aggressive policy and corrupting tendencies of the Roman Catholic Church" and proposed the exclusion from public office of any person who held "civil allegiance, directly or indirectly, to any foreign power, whether civil or ecclesiastical." Favoring the maintenance of undenominational public schools "common to all without dis-

[30] Billington, *The Protestant Crusade, 1800–1860.*
[31] *Ibid.*, 389.

tinction of creed or party," the party insisted that Christianity was in law "an element of our political system." It declared that the Bible, "at once the source of Christianity and the depository and fountain of all civil and religious freedom," should not be excluded from the public schools.[32]

As to other phases of religio-political partisanship, one need only note here the anti-Catholic propaganda of the American Protective Association, or A.P.A., in the eighteen nineties, the Ku Klux Klan of the nineteen twenties, and the injection of the religious issue into the presidential election of 1928. Just how important this factor was in that election, it is hard to say, but it was undoubtedly considerable, especially in the South. Less frequently discussed is the very common exploitation of religious affiliations in local politics. The make-up of a vote-drawing ticket in New York, for instance, is commonly understood to require suitable distribution of elective offices among Protestants, Catholics, and Jews. In short, present-day American politicians still play upon religious sympathies and antagonisms, and no religious group has a monopoly of this vicious kind of partisanship. Bigotry has always been a vice more readily recognized in our opponents than in ourselves and New York need not compare itself too complacently with Tennessee.

On a higher level than such crude appeals to religious prejudice as those just mentioned are the efforts of certain religious groups to influence social legislation. No American church today seriously expects governmental action supporting its theological, or strictly religious, views. Legislative bodies are, however, constantly called upon to deal with problems of social ethics in which members of particular religious communions have a special interest. Some of these ethical principles have, or are believed to have, a significant relation to

[32] Platform in Schmeckebier, *Know Nothing Party in Maryland*, appendix.

religious teaching. So believing, ecclesiastical organizations, or their recognized leaders, have thrown their influence for or against particular measures of legislation.

It is, of course, the Catholic Church that, from the nature of its organization and its conception of authority in matters of faith and morals, finds it easiest to express corporate, as distinguished from individual, opinions on questions falling within what has been called a twilight zone between church and state. That was done, for instance, in certain notable encyclicals of Leo XIII and Pius XI, dealing with such subjects as labor, marriage, and education. Speaking specifically for American Catholics, the second Baltimore Plenary Council (1866) dealt with the ethical aspects of legislation: Such action must always, to be valid, conform to "God's Law." "The Catholic," in the words of this official statement, "has a guide in the Church, as a divine Institution, which enables him to discriminate between what the Law of God forbids or allows; and this authority the State is bound to recognize in its sphere—of moral no less than dogmatic teaching." [33] So, as Father John A. Ryan puts it in his interesting little book, *The Catholic Church and the Citizen*: "With regard to civil laws or proposals for laws which have moral aspects, which involve questions of right and wrong, the Church obviously has the right and the duty to direct the Catholic citizen." [34] It should be remembered that this claim to direct individual members of a religious society in their attitude toward the law of the state is not altogether unique. The Society of Friends has taken a similar attitude on legislation requiring military service or the taking of an oath.

When there is no agreement, even among Christians, as to the ethical aspects of legislation, there arises another question. Conceding the right of any church to enforce its own rules of

[33] Mode, *Source Book*, 472.
[34] P. 40.

conduct as a condition of membership, how far are its members justified in seeking to impose such standards on other persons? One of the most suggestive discussions of this question is that of the late Dr. Figgis. As an Anglo-Catholic member of the Church of England, he favored strict enforcement of its rule against the remarriage of divorced persons; but he also insisted that no attempt should be made to impose this standard by legislation on the community at large. "The Christian law," he said, "is the law of Christians; what may be wise and right for a body of all faiths and every fad is no matter for the Christian Church to decide." [35]

Before the close of the Civil War, the principal social issue on which American churches took, or were asked to take, a stand was the question of slavery. In almost every denomination, however, there were differences of opinion that made united action difficult, or impossible. Definite pronouncements were, however, made by groups representing all shades of opinion from the abolitionist to the proslavery extremists. An interesting statement on this subject is that of the Southern Presbyterians when in 1861 they seceded from the Northern, and largely anti-slavery, wing of that denomination. This statement, issued on behalf of the General Assembly of the Presbyterian Church in the Confederate States of America, declared that legislation on slavery was not the concern of the church, which had "no commission either to propagate or abolish it. The policy of its existence or non-existence" was, it was said, "a question which exclusively belongs to the State." [36] From the point of view of church and state relations, the most significant fact about the slavery issue is not the influence of

[35] J. N. Figgis, *Churches in the Modern State* (London and New York, Longmans, Green and Company), Lecture III, esp. pp. 123–125.

[36] Mode, *Source Book*, 609; E. McPherson, *Political History of the United States during the Great Rebellion* (3 ed., Washington, D. C., 1876), 509–512.

the churches on the policies of state and federal governments, but rather the divisive effect of the political controversy on the churches themselves. Even before secession, the Methodist and Baptist denominations had formed separate organizations on sectional lines, and the withdrawal of the Southern members from the national organization of the Old School Presbyterian Church in 1861 was a natural outcome of the long slavery controversy.[37]

Since the Civil War there have been several issues on which important religious groups have attempted either to secure laws embodying their own ethical standards or to prevent legislation contrary to those standards. Legislation on Sunday observance, or the relaxation of earlier restrictions, may of course be argued on other than religious grounds, closely related as the problem is to the movement for shorter working hours. Religious considerations have undoubtedly been of prime importance in securing older legislation, as well as in recent efforts to keep it on the statute books. On the question of prohibition, there has been no agreement among the churches as a whole. Certain Protestant denominations were closely associated with the Anti-Saloon League in the movement which brought about the Eighteenth Amendment and the Volstead Act. On the question of peace and war, again, the traditional attitude of the Quakers and other definitely pacifist denominations has lately been approached by other religious groups. The problem of the conscientious objector, who does not accept the civic obligation of bearing arms in the national defense, has recently assumed greater relative importance. It is clearly more difficult for governments to deal with strictly individual convictions, when such scruples are not embodied

[37] References on this subject and some illustrative documents are in Mode's *Source Book*, chaps. XXVII and XXVIII. The New School Presbyterians who were almost entirely in the North formed a separate organization in 1857 primarily on theological issues.

in the recognized tenets of corporate religious bodies; in the case of the Quakers, for instance, practical adjustments have usually been made without great inconvenience to the belligerent governments concerned.[38]

At the present moment, and from the point of view of practical politics, three kinds of social legislation—now in force or under discussion—are of special importance to students of religion and the state in America. One of these concerns education and will be discussed later.[39] The other two will be considered briefly at this point. In one group of problems, affecting the institution of the family, powerful forces in our modern life run counter to the dogmatic teaching of certain religious bodies, and especially to that of the most numerous and most strongly organized of the American churches. The other issue, or group of issues, arises more definitely *within* particular churches and is most disturbing to those that inherit the Protestant tradition. The question here is how far churches, as distinguished from their individual members, should take definite positions on matters involving current problems of economic politics, on the ground that this or that economic order is inherently Christian or un-Christian.

In the matter of the family, involving the law of marriage, the Catholic Church has expressed itself clearly, as for example, in the encyclical of Pope Pius XI, "On Christian Marriage," which explicitly condemns modern divorce legislation and "birth control." Furthermore, declarations of the American hierarchy specifically condemn the divorce legislation of the American states.[40] The Baltimore pastoral letter of 1866 held that, "No State law can authorize divorce, so as to

[38] See pp. 136 ff.

[39] See pp. 119 ff.

[40] *Casti Connubii*, December 31, 1930; English text published by National Catholic Welfare Conference (Washington, D. C., 1931).

115

permit the parties divorced to contract new engagements."[41]
So far as civil legislation on any of these subjects is concerned,
and whatever one's personal opinion may be as to its merits or
demerits, it is evident that in certain states the influence of this
church has been effectively exerted in opposition to the relaxation of present legal standards.

On the economic issues arising from more or less radical
proposals looking toward a more nearly collectivist society,
the position of the Catholic Church is quite different from that
of most Protestant bodies. The former, through its highest
authority, has laid down its own principles of economic philosophy.[42] Within certain limits, which exclude on the one side
absolute laissez faire and on the other communism or other
extreme forms of Marxian socialism, there are, of course, differences of opinion within the Church itself. The advocates
of opposing views have their own interpretations and applications of principles laid down by the Vatican. The Papacy itself
is sympathetic with the principle of minimum-wage legislation, partly in the interest of family life. On the other hand, a
large proportion of the Catholic clergy—by no means all—
has opposed the proposed child-labor amendment to the Federal Constitution on the ground that it threatens parental
control of the child and thus weakens the divinely sanctioned
institution of the family.

Among the Protestant denominations the issue is now actively debated whether the present economic system is or is not
so clearly un-Christian that a more collectivist order should

[41] *Concilii Plenarii Baltimorensis*, III (Baltimore, 1866), p. cxiv.

[42] E.g. Encyclicals of Pope Leo XIII (*Rerum Novarum*, May 15, 1891,
"On the Condition of Labor"; English translation in J. J. Wynne, *Great
Encyclical Letters of Pope Leo XIII* [3d ed., 1903, 208–248]); and Pius
XI (*Quadragesimo Anno*, May 15, 1931, "On Social Reconstruction," pub-
lished by National Catholic Welfare Conference, Washington, D. C.,
1931).

be substituted, by *state* action. On the whole question of whether it is the business of the church to adopt a definite economic program there are various attitudes. Some church leaders believe that the Christian gospel embodies—at least in broad outline and by implication—an economic and social philosophy, clearly recognizable as such by all right-minded persons, which should be promoted by the church and made effective through legislation. For some of these persons a truly Christian society would involve some form of collectivism; for others, a considerable modification of the present order in the interest of social justice would best express the Christian ideal. Many persons, on the contrary, regard the churches as agencies for the regeneration of the *individual,* and of society primarily through *individuals* inspired by Christian motives of service. Such persons are skeptical as to the possibility of agreements by men of various temperaments and different mental processes upon any concrete program for a new social order. They, therefore, deprecate efforts by the churches, in their corporate capacities, to influence legislation in a field where ecclesiastical leaders are not necessarily qualified experts, and where equally sincere Christians may not agree on any particular remedy for existing evils.

These are some of the ways in which organized religion has sought, with varying success, to embody its ideals in the action of the state. Certain other phases of the subject can be only mentioned here. There are, for instance, certain international aspects of church and state, including the problems that arise through the missionary activities of American churches—Catholic and Protestant. As citizens, the representatives of American Christianity rely for personal protection upon their home government; to some extent also our government has interested itself in the protection of institutions maintained by missionaries in foreign countries, institutions which—especially in these days of intense nationalism—have been affected by governmental policies in those countries. In other ways also, religious loyalties and antagonisms have complicated international relations; familiar cases in point are the relations of the United States with Soviet Russia, Spain, and Mexico.[43]

Evidently, then, formal "separation" has not always kept religion and politics in watertight compartments, a fact that will become still clearer when we come to consider the relations of church and state in the field of education.

[43] A more recent instance is that of the present German government.

VI

The American Tradition Tested

THE one phase of church and state relations that now seems most likely to present problems of more than merely theoretical interest lies in the field of education. There we have two radically contrasted, not to say irreconcilable, positions. Supporters of the opposing positions are numerous and determined; between them stands, as in most controversies, a middle group, without clearly defined convictions. The two groups that see most clearly what they want are, on the one hand, those who believe that religion should be the integrating principle in education, and those, on the other hand, who emphasize the business of the state under a democratic government to maintain a system of schools open to all children, supported by public taxation, and limiting itself to purely secular instruction.

The first of these two opposing points of view has been effectively stated in certain authoritative pronouncements of the Catholic Church, though it has also considerable support in other religious bodies. Especially significant is the encyclical letter of Pope Pius XI on "The Christian Education of Youth" (December 31, 1929).[1] Conceding that the state had a right to insist on adequate training for citizenship, he nevertheless insisted on the primacy of religion: "first of all education belongs preeminently to the Church, by reason of a double

[1] Translation in *Catholic Educational Review*, March 1930.

title in the supernatural order, conferred exclusively upon her by God Himself; absolutely superior therefore to any other title in the natural order." Furthermore, "every form of instruction no less than every human action, has a necessary connection with man's last end, and therefore cannot be withdrawn from the dictates of the Divine Law, of which the Church is guardian, interpreter and infallible mistress." Education is thus a preparation for membership in a divine society, not merely for life and service in the temporal order. In contrast with the doctrine laid down in this encyclical is the general trend of American educational opinion and legislation since the Revolution. Assuming the special necessity of an educated citizenship in a democratic republic, the American commonwealths have increasingly emphasized the educational function of the state—its obligation to provide schools open to all children and supported by taxes collected from all citizens regardless of church affiliation or creed. In such a system it has seemed essential, in accordance with the general principle of the separation of church and state, that there should be no advocacy of any particular religious creed. Therefore, since no formula has been devised acceptable to all religious groups, it has been thought necessary for the state-supported schools to limit themselves to strictly secular subjects. Religious education is accordingly left to the voluntary efforts of the family, the churches, and private schools under more or less definitely religious auspices.

With these contrasted attitudes in mind, let us consider very briefly the historical background of the present situation. In colonial New England, the prevailing view was that education was a function of the state, but religious considerations had an important part in the establishment of public schools and they were expected to inculcate sound religious ideas, as well as secular knowledge. The coöperation of the clergy was invited, as when, in 1701, a Massachusetts law required the approval of a new schoolmaster in any town by the local minister and at least two others of the neighboring clergy.[2] In Virginia, the state assumed some responsibility for education, but it was regarded as primarily a family concern. There was no system of public schools, and provincial legislation in this field was limited mainly to the care of orphans, apprentices, and other children outside the circle of normal family life; in such legislation provision was made for religious as well as secular instruction.[3] The College of William and Mary in Virginia, like Harvard in Massachusetts, represented the coöperation of church and state in higher education. It was a state college in its origin, chartered by the Crown, and receiving financial support from the provincial assembly, but it was a distinctly Anglican institution. An important educational factor in the South was the work first of Anglican and later of dissenting clergy in whose schools many of the Revolutionary leaders were trained. Significant also is the fact that English schoolmasters, who came to the royal provinces to pursue their calling, were expected to present licenses from the Bishop of London.

In the middle colonies, the provincial governments concerned themselves very little with education, which was left mainly to private initiative or to religious agencies, such as the Anglican Charity School associated with Trinity Church in New York, the schoolmasters of the Society for the Propagation of the Gospel, and the schools maintained in connection with the Dutch Reformed churches. In Pennsylvania, parents were required to provide a modicum of education, which must ensure ability to read the Bible; Quakers and other religious denominations had their own schools. In short, the notion of strictly secular education had little support in colonial times.[4]

[2] Massachusetts Bay, *Acts and Resolves*, I, 470.

[3] M. W. Jernegan, *Laboring and Dependent Classes in Colonial America* (Chicago, 1931), Part III.

[4] Cf. S. W. Brown, *Secularization of American Education*, chaps. I–III.

Perhaps the nearest approach to it was the instruction dispensed by the free-lance teachers in the larger towns. Except for a few Catholics in Maryland and Pennsylvania, the religious teaching provided was that of one or another of the Protestant denominations.

In the Revolutionary era and in the early years of the Republic, there was a growing interest in civic education and, in the case of Jefferson especially, this was associated with a definitely secularizing tendency. In his educational proposals for Virginia, he included some instruction in morals. But he did not favor putting the Bible into the hands of children whose judgments, he said, were "not sufficiently matured for religious inquiries"; instead, they had better learn the most useful facts from history, including that of their own country.[5] It was in accordance with his views that the chair of divinity at the College of William and Mary was abolished. Though Jefferson's plan for public education was too advanced for acceptance even in his own state, it illustrates the beginning of a new outlook. Significant also were the first steps taken in North Carolina and Georgia toward a state system of education.

In New England, as in the North generally, the movement toward the separation of church and state affected education only very gradually. Religious exercises were customary in the public schools and they were intended to be nonsectarian, at least from a Protestant standpoint. More secular textbooks gradually replaced the strongly Protestant *New England Primer*, with its catechism. In 1827, the Massachusetts and New Hampshire legislatures excluded sectarian textbooks [6] from town schools, and in the middle years of the nineteenth century the State School Board, under the leadership of Horace Mann, took a strong stand against sectarian instruc-

[5] *Writings* (Federal ed.), IV, 62.

[6] Brown, *Secularization of American Education*, chap. VII.

tion, though he favored Bible reading.[7] Gradually the tendency toward secularizing public education was strengthened, as the result of foreign immigration which increased the number of families not in sympathy with the older Protestant tradition. Religious exercises which seemed nonsectarian to members of Protestant churches did not seem so to Catholics.

Again, the granting of state funds to denominational schools was felt by many persons to be inconsistent with the theory of separation between church and state. So there came a series of constitutional provisions forbidding such grants. An amendment to this effect was adopted by New Jersey in 1844, and during the next twenty years several other states took similar action.[8] Especially significant was the Massachusetts amendment of 1855, which forbade the appropriation of public school funds, whether state or local, to any schools except those "conducted according to law, under the order and superintendence" of the local public authorities,[9] and specifically prohibited appropriations "to any religious sect for the maintenance exclusively of its own schools." Such prohibitions became general in the later nineteenth century. A good example is the Colorado constitution of 1876, which forbade grants by public authorities to any educational, "literary, or scientific institution controlled by any church or sectarian denomination whatsoever." [10] Reference may be made here to President Grant's unsuccessful effort to incorporate the general principle in a federal amendment.[11]

[7] *Ibid.*, chap. XI.

[8] See the list of states in E. P. Cubberley, *Public Education in the United States* (Boston, 1919), 180. For a good account of the Massachusetts development, see S. M. Smith, *Relation of the State to Religious Education in Massachusetts* (Syracuse, 1926).

[9] Amendment XVIII.

[10] Articles V and VI.

[11] Grant's address to the Army of the Tennessee, 1875, quoted in Moehlman, *American Constitutions and Religion*, 16–17.

By this time there were in the American population three distinct points of view on the question of religious education in the public schools. One group still believed that a nonsectarian form of such teaching was possible. Others, whether definitely secularist or not, believed that under the American system religion could not, or should not, be taught in the public schools. A third position was that of representative Catholics, who would have welcomed public aid to church schools but objected to the kind of religious exercises then customary, including the reading of the King James Bible, which they regarded as Protestant and therefore sectarian.

Especially interesting, with distinct political repercussions, was the schools' controversy in New York City which came to a head about 1840. At that time the City had no real school system of its own; the Public School Society, a private organization of public-spirited citizens, offered schooling for children not otherwise provided for. In addition to private contributions, the Society received public money. Its directors were chiefly drawn from the principal Protestant denominations and some of the more influential members were Quakers; there were, in 1840, some Catholics. Aside from the ordinary common-school branches, the Society provided what were believed to be nonsectarian religious exercises, including the reading of the Bible.

For many years the Society carried on its work successfully and with general approval, but by 1840, the growing Catholic population of the City had radically changed the situation. From the point of view of their church, then vigorously led by Bishop—subsequently Archbishop—Hughes, the instruction then offered by the Society was not really nonsectarian, but definitely Protestant, or irreligious, in tendency. Accordingly, parochial schools had been instituted. However, since they imposed a heavy burden on a comparatively poor constituency composed largely of recent immigrants, it was proposed that part of the state school fund administered by the City should be given to these church schools. In support of this appeal, the Catholic petitioners referred to the Society's use of textbooks believed to misrepresent the historical position of the Catholic Church, as well as to the use of the Protestant, King James, version of the English Bible. Bishop Hughes and his followers also received some support from the Whig governor of the state, William H. Seward, who suggested the establishment of schools where children should have "teachers speaking the same language with themselves and professing the same faith." The Governor's proposal was, however, resented by the strong nativist element in his own party and served only to intensify religious antagonism in city and state politics.

The final outcome of this controversy hardly met the views of either party. The state legislature created a City Board of Education to administer the City schools, and the Public School Society was soon afterwards discontinued. In the new City schools instruction was to be strictly secular, and no school in which "any religious or sectarian doctrine" was "taught, inculcated or practiced" was to receive public funds. Nor was the result satisfactory to Bishop Hughes and his associates, since it definitely excluded the appropriation of public money to parochial schools. Notwithstanding the financial difficulties involved in the expansion of such schools, the program has been vigorously pushed by the Catholic hierarchy. Thus while public education in most communities has become increasingly secular, a comprehensive system of church schools has been built up in New York and in the country at large extending from the elementary grades to the college. Since Catholics, as well as Protestants, are taxed for the support of the secularized public schools, it is hardly surprising that considerable feeling should have developed out of this situation. As the New York Catholics put the case in 1840, parochial schools involve for them "a second taxation, required not by the laws of the land, but the no less imperious demands of their conscience."[12] To the American hierarchy, as to the Papacy, secular education does not seem really neutral in religion. In 1884, the Third Plenary Council of Baltimore urged that Catholic schools should be multiplied "till every Catholic child in the land shall have the means of education within its reach." "To shut religion out of the school, and keep it for home and the Church" was in the opinion of the Council "to train up a generation that will consider religion good for home and the Church, but not for the practical business of real life."[13]

Dissatisfaction with strictly secular· education is not confined to the Catholic Church. The Lutherans also have their parochial schools, though they are far less numerous. In other Protestant denominations, generally speaking, no such development has taken place. There are, of course, private schools that have a distinctly religious character, without formal ecclesiastical connections, but they are not comparable with those of the Catholic and Lutheran churches. In recent years there has been a marked increase in the number and enrollment of parochial schools. The *Official Catholic Directory* for 1939 reported nearly eight thousand Catholic parishes, with schools having an enrollment of more than two million pupils.[14] In view of the very considerable part of the population concerned in the maintenance of such schools, this phase of church and

[12] Bourne, *Public School Society of the City of New York,* chaps. X–XV (with documents); J. R. G. Hassard, *Life of the Most Reverend John Hughes,* chap. XIV.

[13] *Concilii Plenarii Baltimorensis,* III, pp. lxxxiv ff.

[14] Table opposite p. 1069. In addition to the "parish" schools, 441,273 pupils were enrolled in "high schools." This does not include a large number in "academies" for girls.

state relations becomes one of increasing importance, and various solutions have been suggested.

At one extreme we have the suggestion that public policy requires something like a state monopoly of education in the elementary grades. This point of view found expression in the Oregon statute enacted by a popular vote in 1922, which required the attendance at public schools of all children, with minor exceptions, between the ages of eight and sixteen, or until they had completed the studies of the eighth grade. The law was, however, vigorously opposed, and cases arising under it ultimately came before the Supreme Court of the United States. In addition to the institutions immediately involved—including a school of Catholic sisters and a private military academy—other interested groups submitted briefs, including the American Jewish Committee and the Domestic and Foreign Missionary Society of the Protestant Episcopal Church. In support of the statute, the Oregon Attorney General argued that the state had the right to enforce attendance at public schools because of its interest in the training of citizens, "fitted both in body and mind," to perform their civic duties. Furthermore, it was urged that the separation of young children on religious lines was contrary to the best interests of the community and calculated to produce mutual antagonisms and suspicions. These contentions were, however, rejected by the Supreme Court in a memorable opinion delivered by Mr. Justice McReynolds.[15]

The most striking passage in the Oregon decision was that cited by Pius XI in his encyclical letter on "The Christian Education of Youth." This passage, with its defense of parental claims in the education of children as against absolutist theories of the state, is worth quoting: "The fundamental theory of liberty upon which all governments in this Union repose excludes any general power of the state to standardize

[15] 268 U. S. Reports, 510–536.

its children by forcing them to accept instruction from public teachers only. The child is not the mere creature of the state; those who nurture him and direct his destiny have the right, coupled with the high duty, to recognize and prepare him for additional obligations."[16] Whatever may be thought of the decision from a technical legal standpoint, it seems to be generally accepted as establishing a sound public policy.

Before considering certain proposed compromises or adjustments between the supporters of church schools and the existing system of secular public education, it should be said that among Protestants the idea of Bible reading in the schools has not been altogether abandoned, and actual practice varies considerably in this respect. In a few states such reading is definitely required; in others it is made optional with school boards, guided by local public opinion; elsewhere it is specifically forbidden by law or excluded by judicial interpretation of constitutional provisions. Several state courts have held that the reading of the Bible in the King James version without comment is not sectarian instruction; sometimes pupils whose parents object have been excused from such exercises.[17] The practice is, as we have seen, objected to by Catholics, partly on the ground that the King James translation is at some points at variance with church teaching; by Jewish citizens, who object not only to the New Testament but to what they consider the mistranslation or misinterpretation of many passages by Christian translators;[18] by out-and-out secularists; and, finally, by many others who, quite irrespective of their own church connections, are against even the appearance of religious partisanship in publicly supported institutions. In recent years the

[16] *Ibid.*, 535.

[17] A. W. Johnson, *The Legal Status of Church-State Relationships in the United States* (Minneapolis, 1934), 77 ff.

[18] M. J. Kohler, "The Illegality of Bible-Reading in the Schools of New York" (Reprint from *The Jewish Tribune*, June 13, 20, 1930).

trend of opinion would seem to be against such Bible reading. A leading judicial decision on this side was handed down by the Supreme Court of Illinois in 1910 in a suit brought by Catholic parents against a local board of education; the court held that the reading of the Bible in the King James version was sectarian instruction and therefore not permissible in a tax-supported school.[19]

Perhaps the most interesting compromise suggested by a member of the Catholic hierarchy was that of the late Archbishop John Ireland of St. Paul, about fifty years ago. This so-called "Faribault-Stillwater Agreement" was for a few years in actual operation in these Minnesota towns, by arrangement with the local authorities and with the consent of the Vatican. In brief, the plan provided for the leasing of parochial buildings to the school district for use during school hours. The teachers, who were members of a Catholic order, duly certified under the state school law and receiving the ordinary teachers' salaries, gave no religious instruction during school hours, but religious exercises were held before and after those hours in the same buildings. As a result, however, of adverse criticism from Catholics, as well as Protestants, the plan was soon abandoned.[20] In this connection it may be noted that in New York and Pennsylvania the wearing of ecclesiastical garb by teachers has been forbidden; in the latter case by a state law, and in New York by a ruling of the State Department of Education, sustained by the Court of Appeals on the ground that the practice would have a "sectarian" influence.[21]

[19] People *ex. rel.* Ring *et al. v.* Board of Education of District 24 in *Northeastern Reporter*, XCII, 251–266. Cf. the discussion of this subject from different standpoints in Brown, *Secularization of American Education*, chaps. XII and XIII, and Zollmann, *American Church Law*, 93–95.

[20] Documents in Mode *Source Book*, 482–484; A. S. Will, *Life of Cardinal Gibbons* (New York, 1922), chap. XXVIII; Purcell, "John Ireland," in *Dictionary of American Biography*.

[21] Zollmann, *American Church Law*, 99.

Another proposed adjustment is that of releasing a limited amount of school time, during which pupils may receive religious instruction; this practice has been permitted in several states. Under a ruling of the New York State Board of Regents, certain local authorities have in the past permitted such use of school time, and the ruling has been sustained by the Court of Appeals. In 1940, Governor Lehman signed the McLaughlin Bill sanctioning the practice generally, subject to regulations formulated by the Commissioner of Education. This plan has, however, been vigorously opposed in some quarters. A committee of the Civil Liberties Union urged Governor Lehman to veto the McLaughlin Bill on the ground that "cherished American traditions require a complete separation of religious education from public education, and that these traditions are gravely endangered by the McLaughlin Bill." [22]

Other suggestions look to a kind of indirect assistance to church schools. To a certain extent this has always been done through tax exemption, on the ground that education under any auspices should be encouraged. All nonprofit educational institutions, public and private, are thus exempt. More recently, other concessions have been proposed and in some cases adopted. One such measure is the Louisiana law providing that textbooks supplied free of cost to children in the public schools should also be available for pupils in private schools. It was argued in opposition that this was in effect a grant in aid of sectarian schools and therefore unconstitutional; on appeal to the Supreme Court of the United States, the objection was not sustained. Chief Justice Hughes, who delivered the opinion of the court, maintained that the schools were not the beneficiaries of the statute. "The school children and the

[22] *Laws of New York, 1940*, chap. 305; *The New York Times*, April 10, 1940; *The Commonweal*, April 5, 1940; American Civil Liberties Union, *Religious Liberty in the United States Today* (New York, 1939).

state alone are the beneficiaries." It was to be understood, however, that none of the books furnished should be for religious instruction.[23] A similar state concession to parochial schools is the furnishing of free transportation to their pupils, as well as to those attending public schools. This practice would also seem to be covered by the general principle laid down by Chief Justice Hughes in the Louisiana textbook case. A New York statute providing for such transportation was declared unconstitutional by the State Court of Appeals.[24] The Chief Judge of that Court and two other members dissented on much the same ground as that stated in the Louisiana decision; namely, that the aid was not given to the schools but to the children, who were legally entitled to attend them. This issue has now been settled by a constitutional amendment definitely permitting free transportation to children in private and parochial schools.[25]

The principle involved in the supply of textbooks and transportation of pupils in nonpublic schools has lately been endorsed in the *Report of the [President's] Advisory Committee on Education* (1938). The Committee pointed out that "the maintenance of schools under nonpublic auspices results in a significant reduction in public expense." Accordingly, they recommended that federal aid to education through grants for books, transportation, scholarships, and health services be made available to pupils in private as well as public schools.[26] This recommendation has been vigorously attacked by some distinguished professors of education, and it has been defended with equal vigor by President Hutchins, of the University of Chicago, in a recent article in *The*

[23] Moehlman, *American Constitutions and Religion*, 140; 281 U. S. *Reports*, 370 ff., esp. p. 375.

[24] *Judd v. Board of Education*, 278 N. Y. *Reports*, 200–221.

[25] Article XI, sec. 4.

[26] *Report* (Washington, D. C., 1938), 53–54.

Saturday Evening Post.[27] "Since," he argues, "we want all American children to get as good an education as they can, since we know some children will not voluntarily attend public schools, and since we are not prepared to compel them to do so, it is in the public interest to give the states power to use Federal grants to help them go to the schools they will attend and to help make those schools as good as possible." Whatever we may think of the merits of such a policy, it seems probable that discussion of the general issue will continue. It is not, indeed, impossible that the question of more direct aid to private, including parochial, schools may also be actively discussed. Of interest in this connection is an article by Reverend George Johnson, in *The Atlantic Monthly* for April 1940, in which the problem is discussed from the standpoint of a Catholic educator.

One other phase of the church-state problem in education which has been forced on our attention in recent years is the complaint that public-school teaching is often definitely partisan, as against traditional religion and ethics. Assuming that teachers—Catholic, Protestant, or Jewish—must not seek through classroom instruction to indoctrinate their pupils in favor of their respective creeds, it may be asked whether indoctrination of the opposite sort is not equally objectionable. It has been argued that in schools supported by public taxation taxpayers and parents may fairly object to what they regard as propaganda against the religious and ethical convictions of the supporting community. It may be conceded that partisanship, for or against particular religious tenets, is not appropriate in the classroom. Unfortunately, attacks on alleged irreligious teaching have often been so directed by more or less ignorant pressure groups as to menace seriously the intellectual freedom of the teacher. The most familiar illustration of

[27] January 28, 1939; W. H. Kilpatrick in *The Social Frontier*, April 1938.

this is the effort of legislatures and school authorities to prevent free discussion of biological evolution.

The first and best known instance of legislation against the teaching of evolution was that of Tennessee in 1925. A statute of that year made it unlawful for any teacher in any educational institution, supported wholly or in part by public-school funds, "to teach any theory that denies the story of the Divine Creation of man as taught in the Bible, and to teach instead that man has descended from a lower order of animals." Similar laws were enacted in Mississippi and Arkansas. Under the Tennessee law the young Dayton teacher, John T. Scopes, was tried and convicted after a trial marked by the spectacular appearance as opposing counsel of Clarence Darrow for the defense and William J. Bryan for the state. Though the law itself and the verdict of the trial court were upheld by the State Supreme Court, dismissal of the case on a technical ground seems to have precluded an appeal to the Supreme Court of the United States. Two subsequent attempts to repeal the law were decisively beaten. In the absence of specific legislation, the freedom of scientific teaching has also been restricted on religious grounds by state and local school officers. For competent and fair-minded treatment of this subject, with many details which cannot be given here, reference may be made to a recent book prepared for a committee of the American Historical Association by Professor Howard K. Beale, of the University of North Carolina.[28] The author shows that while the more conspicuous and sensational instances of interference with scientific teaching have taken place among the Protestant Fundamentalists of the Southwest, they have by no means been the only offenders; no section of the country can boast a clean record in this respect.

It would seem, then, that more than a century after the for-

[28] *Are American Teachers Free?* (New York, 1936), chap. X. For other forms of religious pressure on the schools, see chap. IX.

mal separation of church and state in the American commonwealths the application of this principle to education still leaves some highly practical problems to be solved.

A monopoly of education by the state is of course one of the chief instruments of totalitarian policy as practised today in Soviet Russia, National Socialist Germany, and Fascist Italy. It is natural, therefore, in closing the present discussion to consider more generally how far the present emphasis on the functions and the authority of the state—an emphasis apparent not only in the contemporary dictatorships but even under more or less democratic constitutions—affects the claims of religion, whether expressed in the decisions of religious bodies or in the personal convictions of individual men and women.

Absolutist theories of the state and its unlimited claim on the obedience of the individual were perhaps never more frankly stated than by Thomas Hobbes in his classic work, the *Leviathan*. Insisting on undivided sovereignty in the state as essential to the maintenance of public order, he held that the sovereign, whether a single person or an assembly, was not "subject to the civil laws." [29] No individual was justified in pleading his religious conviction as a defense against the charge of disobedience to the state. In a Christian commonwealth, only the sovereign could "take notice what is, or what is not, the word of God." [30] In his chapter "Of Power Ecclesiastical," Hobbes illustrated his position by telling the story of Naaman, the Syrian, who was cured of his leprosy by the prophet Elisha, and promised that he would thenceforth serve only the God of Israel. On one point, however, he asked indulgence. When, said Naaman, "my master goeth into the house of Rimmon to worship . . . when I bow down myself in the house of Rimmon, the Lord pardon thy servant in this thing." "This," added Hobbes, "the prophet approved, and bid him,

[29] *Leviathan* (Morley's Library, 1887), Part II, chap. XXVI, p. 124.
[30] *Ibid.*, Part III, chap. XL, p. 213.

'Go in peace.' " The conclusion which Hobbes draws from the Old Testament story is "that whatsoever a subject, as Naaman was, is compelled to do in obedience to his sovereign, and doth it not in order to his own mind, but in order to the laws of his country, that action is not his but his sovereign's."[31] In short, the sovereign being entitled to absolute obedience, the subject must yield his own convictions, so far as external acts are concerned; he need not make a martyr of himself but may plead that the responsibility is not his but his sovereign's.[32]

Hobbes's teaching, in spite of his proof texts from Scripture, could hardly be accepted by any deeply religious person. As we have already seen, Christians of many creeds have agreed that somewhere a line must be drawn between what belongs to Caesar and what belongs to God. However much they may differ as to the precise application of the principle—as to precisely where the line should be drawn—Catholics, Lutherans, Calvinists, and Quakers agree that there is a point at which civil obedience ceases to be a virtue and becomes a sin. Then one must obey God rather than men, though resistance may be passive only. So, Leo XIII in the encyclical, *Libertas Praestantissimum* (1888), speaking of the church but in terms applicable to individuals also, declared: ". . . where a law is enacted contrary to reason, or to the eternal law, or to some ordinance of God, obedience is unlawful, lest, while obeying man, we become disobedient to God. Thus an effectual barrier being opposed to tyranny, the authority in the State will not have all its own way, but the interests and rights of all will be safeguarded." [33] Not less compelling in the minds of the followers of George Fox was their duty to disobey the laws of the state in relation to oaths and the bearing of arms. Father

[31] *Ibid.*, Part III, chap. XLII, pp. 226–227.

[32] *Ibid.*, chap. XLIII, p. 271.

[33] Excerpts in Ryan and Millar, *The State and the Church*, chap. XI, esp. p. 239.

Ryan in his little book on *The Catholic Church and the Citi-zen* indicates cases in which civil disobedience might be justi-fied on the ground that legislation was in violation of natural right. These include the Oregon law directed against parochial schools; hypothetical socialistic legislation, enforced "with utter disregard of property rights"; and even certain provi-sions of the Volstead Act.[34]

Generally speaking, neither of the opposing parties in these conflicts of theory probably desires to push action to its possible logical conclusions. The state has often refrained from meas-ures believed to be within its legitimate jurisdiction, but offen-sive to the religious or ethical sense of respectable citizens. Most religious bodies also would deprecate civil disobedience except when the most vital convictions were involved and the conflict between conscience and law quite unequivocal. In Eng-land and prerevolutionary America, the Anglican Church especially emphasized the duty of obedience to constituted authority, or in extreme cases purely passive refusal of such obedience. Among recent writers of that church, Dr. Figgis has argued, partly on practical grounds: "It is well that most men should regard resistance to laws, however unjust, as practically prohibited by the moral law. If there be 'cases of resistance,' they are best ignored." [35]

At the present time, when the prevailing tendency in the world at large is to magnify the state, we have in the totali-tarian countries something closely approximating the deifica-tion of the Caesars which the early Christians had to face; and there is now no corporate entity comparable with the medieval church to offset the authority of the state. At the same time, mystical or semimystical notions of the national and racial soul—of "blood and soil"—seem to dwarf the indi-vidual personality. In view of this general situation, let us

[34] Pp. 40–42.
[35] *Divine Right of Kings*, 265.

consider more definitely American opinion and practice since the founding of the republic.

The men who voted the Declaration of Independence had no absolutist notions of government. They believed that a state, founded and maintained by the consent of the governed, was not the recipient of absolute authority, even though its powers were to be exercised by representatives of the people. There were "unalienable rights" not surrendered to any government. These were stated in general terms in the Declaration of Independence itself, and more definitely in the bills of rights of the state constitutions. Thus the Virginians, having asserted the principle that there were inherent rights of which men could not "by any compact deprive or divest their posterity," proceeded to enumerate such rights, including, as we have seen, a guarantee of religious liberty. There were lawmakers of that generation who were also willing to waive general provisions of law, out of regard for the religious scruples of Quakers and Mennonites, with respect to the taking of oaths and the bearing of arms. We are not surprised to find such concessions in the first state constitution of the Old Quaker commonwealth. Before 1787 the constitutions of New York, New Hampshire, and Vermont relieved Quakers from the duty of bearing arms. Whether in constitutions or statutes, such Quaker scruples were generally respected, even in the stress of actual warfare, though payments in lieu of military service were commonly required. Of interest in this connection is the Congressional debate on the first ten amendments to the Federal Constitution. One of those proposed by James Madison but not adopted, probably because state action then seemed more appropriate, declared that "no person religiously scrupulous of bearing arms" should be required "to render military service in person." [36]

The first militia law of the United States was adopted in

[36] *Annals of Congress*, First Session, First Congress, I, 434.

1792, after an interesting debate in which the chief points of difference appeared to be whether the privilege of exemption should be paid for, and whether such exemption should be left to the states, the latter course being actually taken. Among the participants in the debates were Roger Sherman of Connecticut and James Madison of Virginia, both members of the Federal Convention and signers of the Constitution. Sherman declared that persons "conscientiously scrupulous of bearing arms could not be compelled to do it"; and Madison, whose opinion carries peculiar weight, wished to include this exemption in the bill. As reported in the *Annals of Congress,* he wished to make the exemption "gratuitous" but thought that impracticable. It was, he said, the glory of this country "that a more sacred regard to the rights of mankind is preserved than has heretofore been known." Aedanus Burke, a member from North Carolina, which had a considerable pacifist element, including Quakers and Moravians, was indignant that such persons should be obliged to pay for the exemption. To do so was, he insisted, "to make a respectable class of citizens pay for a right to a free exercise of their religious principles." Since the First Amendment had just been ratified, he considered such legislation "contrary to the Constitution." [37]

During the first half of the nineteenth century, when the comparatively small-scale War of 1812 and that with Mexico were fought on the basis of voluntary enlistments, the issue raised by the "conscientious objector" seemed largely academic. It ceased to be so during the Civil War when both parties resorted to conscription as the war proceeded. In the North, state practice varied. The Conscription Act of 1864 allowed conscientious objectors of recognized pacifist sects to substitute noncombatant service in the hospitals or in work for the freedmen, on payment of a tax for hospital service. In the Confederacy, individuals belonging to certain religious

[37] *Annals of Congress,* First Congress, II, 1818, 1822, 1824, 1827.

groups were relieved from bearing arms, on providing a substitute or paying a special tax. Many such objectors, however, who refused to take advantage of the permitted alternatives for military service, suffered for their pacifist principles. Some of the leaders on both sides were sympathetic, including Lincoln and Stanton. Lincoln wrote to the widow of a prominent Friend: "For those appealing to me on conscientious grounds, I have done and shall do, the best I could and can, in my own conscience, under my oath to the law." [38]

Before the United States entered the World War, the old militia law was amended by Congressional enactments of 1903 and 1916 exempting from combatant service persons shown to have genuine religious scruples against such service, under regulations prescribed by the President. Under his Executive Order of March 20, 1918, President Wilson developed the policy still further by recognizing not only religious scruples but also "*other* conscientious scruples by them in good faith entertained." [39] Though the higher officials charged with the administration of the Selective Service Act, Secretary Baker and Assistant Secretary Keppel, did what they could to ensure humane treatment of objectors, this could not be said of all members of the recruiting service, and there was undoubtedly some unintelligent and harsh treatment of sincere objectors, who refused on principle to accept even noncombatant service. [40]

[38] A. C. Cole, *Irrepressible Conflict* (New York, 1934), 312–314; A. C. Thomas, *Society of Friends in America* (American Church History Series, VII, New York, 1894), 285–287; E. N. Wright, *Conscientious Objectors in the Civil War* (Philadelphia, 1931); Lincoln, *Complete Works* (ed. New York, 1905), X, 215–216.

[39] U. S. *Statutes at Large*, XXXII, Part I, 775; XXXIX, Part I, 197. There is a summary of the legal situation in the brief of Emily Marx, counsel for defendant in the Bland case (U. S. Supreme Court, Oct. Term, 1930, No. 505).

[40] Norman Thomas, *The Conscientious Objector in America* (New York, 1925).

After the World War, the right to reserve, in the oath of allegiance, conscientious scruples against military service has been discussed in connection with the issue of passports and the applications of aliens for citizenship. In the matter of the passport oath, the Department of State went on record in 1926. When Mr. Roger N. Baldwin, of the Civil Liberties Union, applied for a passport and asked for an official interpretation of the oath to "support and defend the Constitution," he was informed by the Chief of the Passport Division that the Department saw no reason why a nonresistant should not take it; if, however, he still had scruples, the Department would consider a formal application with the qualifying clause, "so far as my conscience will allow." [41] In contrast with this action of the Department of State has been the treatment of essentially the same principle in connection with the naturalization of aliens. Under this head, we may confine ourselves to three leading cases: those of *United States v. Schwimmer, United States v. Macintosh,* and *United States v. Bland.* Though no two of these cases were exactly alike, all three of the individuals involved, when examined for naturalization, were rejected because of conscientious scruples which prevented them from giving an unqualified declaration of their readiness to bear arms in the national defense. In each case the demand for such a declaration appeared somewhat academic; two of the three applicants were women, who have never been required to bear arms, while the third was past the normal limit of military service.

Madame Rosika Schwimmer was a Hungarian by nationality, forty-nine years of age, and a well-known pacifist lecturer and writer. On applying for citizenship in 1927, she agreed to take the customary oath of allegiance, but on examination in the Federal District Court at Chicago she explained that she was "willing to do anything that an American citi-

[41] Copy of this letter in the Marx brief above mentioned.

zen is called upon to do," except fight, and "would recognize the right of the Government to deal with her as it dealt with its male citizens who for conscientious reasons refuse to take up arms." She admitted that she was an uncompromising pacifist and her application was rejected specifically on that ground. The case was then reviewed by the Court of Appeals, which, reversing the decision of the District Court, directed the approval of Madame Schwimmer's petition; "mere views" were not, under the statute, a sufficient ground for denying citizenship. Her sex and age were also taken into account. There was no reason to suppose that a woman would ever be called to bear arms, and her rights were "not to be determined by putting conundrums to her." [42] From the decision of this second court, the Government appealed to the Supreme Court where the decision of the Court of Appeals was reversed and that of the District Court sustained. Madame Schwimmer was accordingly denied citizenship. The Government held that "religious scruples" were not involved, since she "had no religion." The action of the Supreme Court was not, however, unanimous; three of the nine justices dissented, including the two most distinguished lawyers on the court, Justices Holmes and Brandeis. In his dissenting opinion Justice Holmes made his well-known plea for "freedom for the thought that we hate." He could not share the pacifist optimism of Madame Schwimmer, although he suggested that the Quakers had "done their share to make the country what it is." "I had not," he continued, "supposed hitherto that we regretted our inability to expel them because they believe more than some of us do in the teachings of the Sermon on the Mount." [43]

[42] 27 *Federal Reporter* (2), 742–744.

[43] *United States v. Schwimmer*, 279 U. S. *Reports*, 644–655; American Civil Liberties Union, *The Case of Rosika Schwimmer* (New York, June 1929).

The case of Marie Bland, a Canadian-born applicant, differed from that of Madame Schwimmer in that she pleaded definitely religious scruples. A member of the Episcopal Church, she held that war was un-Christian and therefore she could not take up arms. A nurse by profession, she had served the American Expeditionary Forces in France and was willing to give service in a future war, even, if necessary, on the firing line; the Government admitted that, except on this issue of willingness to bear arms, she was fully qualified for citizenship. In her case, a special brief was submitted on behalf of several prominent clergy of the American Episcopal Church including three bishops. Miss Bland's application was denied by the District Court in New York; but, as in the case of Madame Schwimmer, the Circuit Court of Appeals reversed the decision, holding that the petitioner had indicated "a willingness to assume all the obligations and duties of citizenship as required by the Constitution and the laws of the country." Again, however, the Government appealed to the Supreme Court, which affirmed the original decision of the District Court, in refusing naturalization.[44]

The decision in Miss Bland's case was brief, and the issues involved were covered more fully in the court's decision in *United States v. Macintosh*, handed down at the same time. Dr. Douglas Clyde Macintosh, a professor in the Yale Divinity School, had been a chaplain in the Canadian army with service at the front and subsequently had charge of an American Y.M.C.A. hut on the Saint-Mihiel front. He was not a thoroughgoing pacifist and was willing to take the usual oath as he understood it; but made the following statement: "I am *not* willing to promise beforehand, and without knowing the cause for which my country may go to war, either that I will

[44] *United States v. Bland*, 283 U. S. *Reports*, 636–637; briefs by E. Marx, as counsel for Miss Bland, and for E. L. Parsons, *et al. Amici Curiae* (U. S. Supreme Court, Oct. Term 1930, No. 505).

or that I will not 'take up arms in defense of this country,' however 'necessary' the war may seem to be to the government of the day." He explained that "he was willing to give to the United States, in return for citizenship, all the allegiance he ever had given or ever could give to any country, but that he could not put allegiance to the Government of any country before allegiance to the will of God." [45]

As in the Schwimmer and Bland cases, Professor Macintosh's application was rejected by the District Court, approved by the Circuit Court of Appeals, and finally refused by the Supreme Court. The case is notable because of the issue involved, the distinguished counsel, including John W. Davis, a former Solicitor General of the United States, and the bare majority of five to four by which the decision was rendered. Counsel for Macintosh argued that the Constitution and laws of the United States did not "require that citizens with conscientious scruples should bear arms"; that the Naturalization Act itself made no such requirement; that the federal and state governments had for a century and a half actually exempted persons who had religious scruples from combatant service; that it was unfair to require as a condition of naturalization a promise to forgo a privilege enjoyed by native-born citizens under the Constitution and laws.

Justice Sutherland, delivering the opinion of the court, brushed aside these contentions of counsel. The statements made by Professor Macintosh were held to be quite incompatible with the oath of allegiance. Concessions made to conscientious objectors in time of war were *privileges* conferred by Congress at its discretion and not *rights* which could be claimed against the practically absolute authority of Congress

[45] *United States v. Macintosh*, 283 U. S. *Reports*, 605–635; brief of J. W. Davis, C. E. Clark, and Allen Wardwell, Counsel, U. S. Supreme Court, Oct. Term, 1930, No. 504. The proceedings in the Circuit Court of Appeals are in 42 *Federal Reporter* (2), 845–849.

under the war power. In effect, the court held that Professor Macintosh proposed "to make his own interpretation of the will of God the decisive test which shall conclude the government and stay its hand." "We are," continued Justice Sutherland, "a Christian people . . . acknowledging with reverence the duty of obedience to the will of God"; but he insisted that the government could not safely proceed, except on the assumption "that *unqualified* obedience to the Nation and submission and obedience to the laws of the land, as well those made for war as those made for peace, are not inconsistent with the will of God." This opinion was concurred in by Justices Butler, McReynolds, Roberts, and Van Devanter.

This majority decision of the Supreme Court establishes for the time being the principle that conscientious scruples against military service preclude admission to citizenship. It would seem to prevent the naturalization hereafter of such persons, hitherto considered eligible, as members of the Society of Friends, the Mennonite Church, and other pacifist sects. Nevertheless the moral, if not the legal, force of the decision is inevitably affected by the number and distinction of the dissenting judges—Chief Justice Hughes and Associate Justices Holmes, Brandeis, and Stone. The Chief Justice himself delivered the dissenting opinion; and few students of our legal history would deny that in point of intellectual distinction the superiority was distinctly on the side of the dissenting justices. The Chief Justice pointed out that the oath expected of applicants for naturalization was essentially the same as that required on taking public office. That oath should, he held, "be read in the light of our regard from the beginning for freedom of conscience. While it has always been recognized that the supreme power of governments may be exerted and disobedience to its commands may be punished, we know that with many of our worthy citizens it would be a heart-searching question if they were asked whether they would promise to obey a law believed to be in conflict with religious duty." An interpretation of the official oath that would exclude such persons would, he believed, be "generally regarded as contrary not only to the specific intent of the Congress but as repugnant to the fundamental principles of representative government." The same principle would, he held, apply to the naturalization oath. In another part of this opinion, the Chief Justice seems to reach the heart of the great issue we are considering. It is worth quoting and remembering: "Much has been said of the paramount duty to the State, a duty to be recognized, it is urged, even though it conflicts with convictions of duty to God. Undoubtedly that duty to the State exists *within the domain of power*,[46] for governments may enforce obedience to laws regardless of scruples. . . . But in the forum of conscience, duty to a moral power higher than the State has always been maintained. The reservation of that supreme obligation, as a matter of principle, would unquestionably be made by many of our conscientious and law-abiding citizens."

This is surely an admirable statement by a great public servant who can certainly not be charged with advocating a lawless individualism, or with lack of regard for the legitimate claims of the state upon its citizens. Of course, no simple formula can really solve the problem as it may at any time present itself to the individual conscience. A humane and flexible type of statesmanship like that of Mr. Hughes may well avert in most cases the ultimate test; but there will always be the possibility of a situation in which the religious-minded person will have to choose between submission to the coercive power of a state, which acknowledges no limitation upon its authority, and the demands of his own conscience. On both sides of the dilemma, we have to do with fallible human nature, whether in the individual or in the rulers of the state.

[46] Italics mine.

Bibliographical Notes

I. OLD WORLD TRADITIONS

The titles listed in this and later chapters include only a few even of the more important works dealing with the topics discussed but they may serve as a guide to more intensive studies.

MEDIEVAL THEORY AND PRACTICE. For briefer treatments of church and state theories in the Middle Ages, see W. A. Dunning, *A History of Political Theories, Ancient and Medieval* (New York, 1902), chaps. V–X; *The Cambridge Medieval History* (Cambridge, England, and New York, 1911–1936), especially Vol. VI, chaps. XVI and XVIII, and Vol. VIII, chap. XX; J. N. Figgis, *Divine Right of Kings* (2d ed., Cambridge, England, Cambridge University Press, 1922), chaps. I–IV. The most extensive treatment is in R. W. and A. J. Carlyle, *A History of Mediaeval Political Theory in the West* (6 vols., New York, Edinburgh, and London, 1903–1936). A standard Catholic authority on church and state is F. J. Moulart, *L'Église et l'État* (2d ed., Paris, 1879). Church and state ideas in their relation to the general concept of sovereignty are discussed in Otto Gierke, *Political Theories of the Middle Age* (an English translation by F. W. Maitland, with an introduction by the translator, Cambridge, England, 1900). Compare also, for the medieval tradition and later developments, E. Troeltsch, *The Social Teaching of the Christian Churches* (English translation, 2 vols., New York, 1931).

EARLY MODERN THEORY AND PRACTICE. For the era of the Protestant Revolution and the Religious Wars, the following are useful: J. W. Allen, *Political Thought in the Sixteenth Century* (London, 1928); W. A. Dunning, *A History of Politi-*

cal Theories, from Luther to Montesquieu (New York, 1921),
especially chaps. I–IV; J. N. Figgis, *Divine Right of Kings,* his
Studies of Political Thought from Gerson to Grotius (Cambridge, England, 1923), and his chapter in the *Cambridge Modern History,* III, chap. XXII; Lord Acton, *The History of
Freedom and Other Essays* (London, 1907); Preserved Smith,
A History of Modern Culture, I (New York, 1930), Part III,
"Social Control"; Francesco Ruffini, *Religious Liberty* (London,
1912), preface by J. B. Bury. A good brief discussion of Calvinism is that of Fairbairn in *Cambridge Modern History,* II, chap.
XI. There are standard biographies of Calvin by E. Doumergue
(French Protestant), F. W. Kampschulte (German Catholic),
and Williston Walker; Walker's *John Calvin* (New York,
1906) is the best available in English. There are useful studies
by H. D. Foster in his *Collected Essays* (privately printed,
1929), especially "Calvin's Programme for a Puritan State in
Geneva" (reprinted from *The Harvard Theological Review,*
October 1908). The primary source for Calvin's theory is, of
course, his *Institutes of the Christian Religion,* especially Book
IV, chap. XX. The English translation here cited is that of
H. Beveridge (3 vols., Edinburgh, 1846).

Anglican and Puritan Theory on the Eve of Coloni-
zation. The most useful single work is that of W. K. Jordan,
in three books, under the general title of *The Development of
Religious Toleration in England* (Cambridge, Massachusetts,
Harvard University Press, 1932–1938). The first covers the
Tudor period and the later volumes carry the narrative to the
Restoration; there are extensive lists of primary and secondary
works. For the Elizabethan settlement of the Anglican Church,
see A. F. Pollard, *Political History of England, 1558–1603*
(London, 1915), especially chaps. XI and XIX; and W. H.
Frere, *History of the English Church, 1558–1625* (London,
1904), especially chaps. II and III. On the legal aspects of the
establishment there is an excellent summary in F. W. Maitland,

Constitutional History of England (Cambridge, England, 1913), 506–526; the subject is more fully treated in F. Makower, *Constitutional History and Constitution of the Church of England* (London, 1895). The principal documents are collected in J. R. Tanner, *Tudor Constitutional Documents* (Cambridge, England, Cambridge University Press, 1922); H. Gee and W. J. Hardy, *Documents Illustrative of English Church History* (London, 1896); and S. R. Gardiner, *Constitutional Documents of the Puritan Revolution* (Oxford, England, Clarendon Press, 1889). The ablest defense of the Anglican system in this period is Richard Hooker's *Ecclesiastical Polity*, Book VIII; the best edition is in his *Works*, edited by John Keble and others (3 vols., 1888). Various shades of Puritan opinion are dealt with in Jordan's volumes, where the chief sources are indicated.

II. EUROPEAN IDEAS TRANSPLANTED

NON-ENGLISH COLONIES. For church and state relations in the Spanish, French, and Dutch colonies, see the following: B. Moses, *Spanish Dependencies in South America* (2 vols., New York, 1914), chap. XII; J. L. Mecham, *Church and State in Latin America* (Chapel Hill, North Carolina, 1934); F. Parkman, *Old Regime in Canada* (various editions), Part II, chap. IV; Mack Eastman, *Church and State in Early Canada* (Edinburgh, 1915); W. A. Riddell, *The Rise of Ecclesiastical Control in Quebec* (New York, 1916); H. L. Osgood, *American Colonies in the Seventeenth Century* (New York, 1904), II, 333–335, a good summary for New Netherland; E. T. Corwin, *A History of the Reformed Church, Dutch*, in American Church History Series, VIII; Frederick J. Zwierlein, *Religion in New Netherland* (Rochester, 1910), from a Catholic standpoint. The documents are collected in H. Hastings, ed., *Ecclesiastical Records. State of New York*, I (Albany, 1901).

ANGLICAN SYSTEM. The best account of the Anglican establishment in early Virginia is in P. A. Bruce, *Institutional History of Virginia in the Seventeenth Century* (2 vols., New York, 1910), Vol. I, Part I. Essential documents are in Alexander Brown, *Genesis of the United States* (2 vols., Boston, 1890); W. W. Hening, *Virginia . . . Statutes at Large . . .,* Vols. I and II; in W. S. Perry, *Papers Relating to the History of the Church in Virginia* (Hartford, 1870); cf. his *History of the American Episcopal Church* (2 vols., Boston, 1885), Vol. I. A convenient selection of documents is in P. G. Mode, *Source Book and Bibliographical Guide for American Church History* (Menasha, Wisconsin, 1921), chap. II. For relations with the episcopate in England, see A. L. Cross, *Anglican Episcopate and the American Colonies* (New York, 1902; reissue, Cambridge, Massachusetts, 1924). For the ecclesiastical authority of the royal governors, see E. B. Greene, *Provincial Governor* (New York, 1898), 128–132, and L. W. Labaree, *Royal Instructions to British Colonial Governors* (2 vols., New York, 1935), Part XII.

Puritan System in New England. The material is abundant and much of it highly controversial. The following are a few of the more important titles: H. L. Osgood, *American Colonies in the Seventeenth Century,* I (New York, 1904), Part II, chaps. II–V (an excellent account of the Massachusetts theocracy); C. M. Andrews, *The Colonial Period of American History,* I (New Haven, 1934); Perry Miller, *Orthodoxy in Massachusetts,* 1630–1650 (Cambridge, Massachusetts, 1933), especially chaps. VII and VIII. There are vigorous onslaughts on the Puritan system in C. F. Adams, *Three Episodes of Massachusetts History,* Vol. I (Boston, 1892), and in J. T. Adams, *Founding of New England* (Boston, 1921). There is a more sympathetic treatment of the Puritan leaders in S. E. Morison's *Builders of the Bay Colony* (Boston, 1930). Governor Thomas Hutchinson's *History of the Colony and Province of Massachusetts-bay,* Vol. I (first published in 1764 but now available in an excellent modern edition, edited by L. S. Mayo, Cambridge, Massachusetts, 1936); chap. IV is written from the standpoint of an eighteenth-century Puritan of liberal tendency in religious matters. For Connecticut and New Haven, see M. L. Greene, *Religious Liberty in Connecticut* (Boston, 1905) and I. M. Calder, *The New Haven Colony* (New Haven, 1934). There is also an older general survey of New England as a whole in P. E. Lauer, *Church and State in New England* (Johns Hopkins University Studies, X, Nos. 2 and 3).

PURITAN SOURCES. An excellent selection of the more important documents is available in P. Miller and T. H. Johnson, *The Puritans* (New York, American Book Company, 1938), with useful introductions to each group of documents; note especially chap. II, "The Theory of the State and of Society." There are briefer selections in P. G. Mode, *Source Book and Bibliographical Guide for American Church History*, chaps. IV–VI; and A. B. Hart, *American History Told by Contemporaries*, I, chaps. XV–XVIII. The Cambridge Platform of 1648, representing the official theory of the Massachusetts churches, is in W. Walker, *Creeds and Platforms of Congregationalism* (New York, 1893.). The government position is set forth in "The Body of Liberties" of Massachusetts (available in W. A. Macdonald, *Select Charters*, New York, 1899, No. 17) and in the recently discovered *Book of the General Lawes and Libertyes Concerning the Inhabitants of the Massachusetts* (1648; reprint, Cambridge, Massachusetts, 1929). The ideas of Governor John Winthrop may be studied in J. K. Hosmer, ed., *Winthrop's Journal* (2 vols., New York, 1908) and in R. C. Winthrop, *Life and Letters of John Winthrop* (2d ed., 2 vols., Boston, 1869). A picturesque illustration of Puritan thinking is Edward Johnson's *Wonderworking Providence of Sion's Saviour in New England*, first published in 1653 and recently edited by J. F. Jameson (New York, 1910). Nathaniel Ward's *Simple Cobler of Aggawam in America*, first published in 1647, was an aggressive argument against toleration; see Miller and Johnson, *The Puritans*, 225–236. For the pertinent clauses of the Connecticut

"Fundamental Orders" and the "Fundamental Articles" of New Haven Colony, see *Public Records of the Colony of Connecticut,* I, 20–25, and *New Haven Colonial Records* (excerpts from both in Macdonald, *Select Charters*).

III. LIBERALIZING FACTORS IN COLONIAL AMERICA

ROGER WILLIAMS AND THE RHODE ISLAND EXPERIMENT. A good summary of Williams's conflict with the Massachusetts theocracy is in H. L. Osgood, *American Colonies in the Seventeenth Century,* I, 224–235. Firsthand evidence for his activities in Massachusetts is scanty—mainly references in *Winthrop's Journal* and Williams's later writings. Of the numerous biographies of Williams, the most recent is S. H. Brockunier, *The Irrepressible Democrat: Roger Williams* (New York, 1940). In general, biographers have been sympathetic and not always critical, but H. M. Dexter, *As to Roger Williams* (Boston, 1876), was sharply critical. A recent discussion is J. E. Ernst, *Political Thought of Roger Williams* (Seattle, 1929). Serious students of Williams should go to his own writings in the *Publications* of the Narragansett Club (6 vols., Providence, 1866–1874). For the Rhode Island record in general, see I. B. Richman, *Rhode Island, Its Making and Its Meaning* (2 vols., New York, 1902). The official documents are in Rhode Island Colony *Records* (10 vols., Providence, 1856–1865), I and II, and in H. M. Chapin, *Documentary History of Rhode Island* (2 vols., Providence, 1916–1919).

CHURCH AND STATE IN THE PROPRIETARY PROVINCES. The best general discussion is in H. L. Osgood, *American Colonies in the Seventeenth Century,* II, chap. XIII. The charters to the proprietors and the "Fundamental Constitutions" of Carolina are in B. P. Poore's *Federal and State Constitutions, Colonial Charters,* etc., and in F. N. Thorpe's enlarged edition of that compilation.

MARYLAND. C. C. Hall, *Narratives of Early Maryland*

(New York, 1910) brings together important documents, including an English translation of the royal charter, Lord Baltimore's instructions (1633), and the "Act Concerning Religion" (1649). There are other relevant documents in B. T. Johnson, *Foundations of Maryland* (in Maryland Historical Society *Fund Publications*, No. 18). The special student will go to the official records published in the *Archives of Maryland* (Baltimore, Maryland Historical Society, 1883–), including the proceedings of the Council and Assembly. There is a good account of the church-state situation in N. D. Mereness, *Maryland as a Proprietary Province* (New York, 1910), Part II, chap. VII. Much of the extensive literature of the subject, Protestant and Catholic, is controversial. For a scholarly Catholic presentation, see J. G. Shea, *Catholic Church in Colonial Days* (New York, 1886; Vol. I of his *Catholic Church in the United States*). There is an excellent critical treatment of the subject in C. M. Andrews, *Colonial Period of American History*, II (New Haven, 1936), chaps. VIII and IX.

PENNSYLVANIA. A standard old life of Penn is S. M. Janney's *Life of William Penn* (6th ed., Philadelphia, 1882), and there are several modern biographies. See W. I. Hull, *Eight First Biographies of William Penn* (Swarthmore, Pennsylvania, 1936), his *William Penn, a Topical Biography* (New York, 1937), and the critical note in C. M. Andrews, *Colonial Period*, III (New Haven, 1937), 270–271. A recent discussion of Penn's theories is E. C. O. Beatty, *William Penn as Social Philosopher* (New York, 1939). For church and state policies in Pennsylvania, see W. R. Shepherd, *Proprietary Government in Pennsylvania* (New York, 1896), especially Part II, chaps. I, IV, VII, XII; I. Sharpless, *Quaker Experiment in Government*, Vol. I (Philadelphia, 1902), from a Quaker standpoint; and W. T. Root, *The Relations of Pennsylvania with the British Government* (New York, 1912), especially chaps. VIII–X. The successive "Frames of Government" and the "Charter of

Privileges" issued by Penn to his province in 1701 are in B. P. Poore, *Federal and State Constitutions*, etc. For one of Penn's early drafts of a system for Pennsylvania, see the "Fundamental Constitutions" in *Pennsylvania Magazine of History and Biography* (The Historical Society of Pennsylvania), XX, 283–301. The Great Law of 1682 and other important documents are in the *Charter to William Penn, and Laws of the Province of Pennsylvania* (Harrisburg, 1879).

THE CAROLINA PROPRIETORS. The provisions relating to religion in the royal charter of 1663, the "Concessions and Agreements" of 1665, and the "Fundamental Constitutions" of 1669 are in the *Colonial Records of North Carolina*, I. Subsequent developments may be studied in E. McCrady, *History of South Carolina under the Proprietary Government* (New York, 1897), and two essays by S. B. Weeks: *The Religious Development in the Province of North Carolina* in Johns Hopkins University Studies, Series X, and *Church and State in North Carolina* (*ibid.*, Series XI).

ENGLISH POLICIES IN THE LATER SEVENTEENTH CENTURY. For a brief account of the English background, see G. N. Clark, *The Later Stuarts* (Oxford, 1934). The chief statutory provisions relating to religion during this period are collected in C. G. Robertson, *Select Statutes, Cases and Documents* (London and New York, 1904); especially important for the colonies is the Toleration Act of 1689 (see Robertson, 70–75). For a summary of the laws affecting dissenters, see F. W. Maitland's *Constitutional History*, 515–519. British policy in relation to religion in the colonies from 1670 on may be traced in L. W. Labaree's *Royal Instructions to Colonial Governors*, II, Part XII. The religious factors in the colonial revolution of 1688–1689 must be studied mainly in the history of particular colonies, but they are also treated in H. L. Osgood, *American Colonies in the Seventeenth Century*, III, and Edward Channing's *History of the United States*, II. An important collection of sources is C. M. Andrews, ed., *Narratives of the Insurrections* (New York, 1915).

DEVELOPMENTS AFTER 1689. An excellent summary is in Edward Channing, *History of the United States,* II, chap. XV. H. L. Osgood, *American Colonies in the Eighteenth Century* (4 vols., New York, 1924–1925), Vols. II and III, has important chapters on church-state developments, including one on the "Great Awakening." For the colonial attitude toward Catholics, see Sister M. Augustina (Ray), *American Opinion of Roman Catholicism in the Eighteenth Century* (New York, 1936). Local Studies: S. M. Reed, *Church and State in Massachusetts, 1691–1740* (Urbana, Illinois, 1914); J. C. Meyer, *Church and State in Massachusetts* (Cleveland, 1930); M. L. Greene, *Religious Liberty in Connecticut*; N. D. Mereness, *Maryland,* 435–457; H. J. Eckenrode, *Separation of Church and State in Virginia* (Richmond, 1910); M. W. Jernegan, "Religious Toleration and Freedom in Virginia" in A. C. McLaughlin, *et al., Source Problems in United States History* (New York, 1918), No. IV, with select bibliography; R. C. Strickland, *Religion and the State in Georgia* (New York, 1939); and the North Carolina studies by S. B. Weeks, noted above, p. 154.

IV. "SEPARATION"

A useful manual for the Revolutionary era is E. F. Humphrey, *Nationalism and Religion in America, 1774–1789* (Boston, 1924), which has an extensive bibliography and numerous extracts from the sources. There is a suggestive brief discussion in J. F. Jameson, *The American Revolution Considered as a Social Movement* (Princeton, 1926), chap. IV.

THE CHURCHES AND THE REVOLUTIONARY MOVEMENT. For a general view, see C. H. Van Tyne, "Influence of the Clergy and of Religious and Sectarian Forces on the American Revolution" in *American Historical Review,* XIX, 44–64, or his *Causes of the American Revolution* (Boston, 1922), chap.

XIII. The best treatment of the Anglican episcopate controversy is in A. L. Cross, *Anglican Episcopate and the American Colonies* (with documents); for interesting correspondence on this and related topics, see H. and C. Schneider, eds., *Samuel Johnson . . . His Career and Writings*, I (New York, 1929). See also W. S. Perry, *History of the American Episcopal Church* (2 vols., Boston, 1885), his *Historical Collections relating to the American Colonial Church* (5 vols., Hartford, 1870–1878), and the *Documentary History of the Protestant Episcopal Church in the United States* (edited by him with F. L. Hawks, and relating more particularly to Connecticut, 2 vols., New York, 1863–1864). The New England Puritan outlook may be studied in Alice Baldwin, *The New England Clergy and the American Revolution* (Durham, North Carolina, 1928); typical political sermons are collected in J. W. Thornton, *Pulpit of the American Revolution* (Boston, 1860). For the similar Presbyterian attitude, see C. A. Briggs, *American Presbyterianism*, chap. IX. The Quaker problem is sympathetically presented in I. Sharpless, *Quaker Experiment in Government* (Philadelphia, 1898), Part II. For anti-Catholic feeling as a factor and the position of the Catholics generally during this period, see Sister M. Augustina (Ray), *American Opinion of Roman Catholicism*; J. G. Shea, *Life and Times of the Most Reverend John Carroll* (New York, 1888); and P. Guilday, *Life and Times of John Carroll* (2 vols., New York, 1922).

THE PROCESSES OF SEPARATION. Provisions in the early state constitutions are in the collections by B. P. Poore and F. N. Thorpe. Most of the pertinent clauses are assembled in C. H. Moehlman, *The American Constitutions and Religion* (Berne, Indiana, 1938). The subject is briefly discussed in Edward Channing, *History of the United States*, III, 560–566; in an earlier compilation by I. A. Cornelison, *Relation of Religion to Civil Government in the United States* (New York, 1895); and in A. Nevins, *The American States, 1775–1789* (New York,

1924), 420–441. The fullest treatment of the development in Virginia is in H. J. Eckenrode, *The Separation of Church and State in Virginia.* There is a good summary in C. R. Lingley, *Transition in Virginia from Colony to Commonwealth* (New York, 1910), 190–211. W. M. Gewehr, *Great Awakening in Virginia* (Durham, North Carolina, 1930) throws light on the influence of the "popular churches." Excerpts from the sources are collected by M. W. Jernegan, in A. C. McLaughlin, *et al.*, *Source Problems in United States History*, No. IV. See also C. F. James, *Documentary History of the Struggle for Religious Liberty in Virginia* (Lynchburg, Virginia, 1900). The Virginia Statute of Religious Liberty is in W. W. Hening's *Statutes*, XII, 84–86, and in S. E. Morison, *Sources and Documents Illustrating the American Revolution,* 206–208. The biographies and correspondence of Jefferson and Madison are of special importance for this topic. On the struggle for disestablishment in New England, 1780–1833, see J. C. Meyer, *Church and State in Massachusetts, 1740–1833;* M. L. Greene, *Religious Liberty in Connecticut;* R. J. Purcell, *Connecticut in Transition* (Washington, D. C., 1918). J. F. Thorning's *Religious Liberty in Transition, New England* (New York, 1931) is written from a Catholic standpoint. There are brief suggestive discussions in W. A. Robinson, *Jeffersonian Democracy in New England* (New Haven, 1916), chap. V; and A. B. Darling, *Political Changes in Massachusetts, 1824–1848* (New Haven, 1925). For the influence of the Baptists as advocates of complete separation, see I. Backus, *History of New England, with Particular Reference to . . . Baptists* (a contemporary work, reprinted with notes, 2 vols., Newton, Massachusetts, 1871); and A. Hovey, *Memoir of . . . the Reverend Isaac Backus* (Boston, 1859).

ECCLESIASTICAL ORGANIZATION AS AFFECTED BY INDEPENDENCE AND FEDERAL UNION. There are general surveys in Humphrey's *Nationalism and Religion*, Part II, with numerous references, and J. F. Jameson, *Essays in the Constitutional History of the United States . . . 1775–1789* (Boston, 1889), chap. III. For developments in particular churches, see the volumes in the American Church History series. For the denominations in which such changes were especially important, see, for the Catholics, the lives of Bishop Carroll by J. G. Shea and P. Guilday; for the Protestant Episcopal Church, A. L. Cross's *Anglican Episcopate and the American Colonies*, chap. XII and Appendix XIV, and W. S. Perry's *American Episcopal Church*; for the Presbyterians, C. A. Briggs, *American Presbyterianism*, 354–373; for the Methodists, A. Stevens, *History of the Methodist Episcopal Church in the United States* (4 vols., 1864–1867).

v. after "separation"

General Works on Recent and Contemporary Church-State Problems in the United States. For a useful introduction, with select references, see W. A. Brown, *Church and State in Contemporary America* (New York, 1938), prepared for a committee of the Federal Council of the Churches of Christ in America. For the Catholic position on many problems, see J. A. Ryan and M. F. X. Millar, *The State and the Church* (New York, The Macmillan Company, 1924), prepared for the National Catholic Welfare Council and especially adapted to American readers; much of the same material is in *Catholic Principles of Politics* by John A. Ryan and Francis J. Boland (New York, 1940). Dr. Ryan has also written a suggestive popular essay on *The Catholic Church and the Citizen* (New York, The Macmillan Company, 1928). See also *The Catholic Encyclopaedia* (16 vols., New York, 1907–1914). In his *Roman Catholic Church in the Modern State* (New York, Dodd, Mead and Company, 1928), the late Charles C. Marshall presented a vigorous critique of the Catholic position as stated by Dr. Ryan and other American spokesmen. The most comprehensive treatment of church-state relations in their legal aspects, with citation of judicial decisions, is Carl Zollmann's *American Church Law* (St. Paul, 1933), a revised and enlarged edition of his *American Civil Church Law* (New York, 1917). For this, as for preceding chapters, P. G. Mode's *Source Book and Bibliographical Guide for American Church History* (Menasha, Wisconsin, Banta Publishing Company, 1921) is a useful work of reference. Essential sources for Catholic teaching are the Papal encyclicals; a convenient guide to the more recent of these pronouncements is Sister M. C. Carlen, *A Guide to the Encyclicals of the Roman Pontiffs from Leo XIII to the Present Day* (New York, 1939). See especially English translations in J. J. Wynne, *The Great Encyclical Letters of Pope Leo XIII* (3d ed., New York, 1908), and the series issued for the pontificate of Pius XI by the National Catholic Welfare Conference (Washington, D. C., 1926–1937).

RELIGION AND PARTY POLITICS. The subject is briefly treated, in connection with nativism, in several of the general histories of the United States. It receives considerable attention in J. B. McMaster's *History of the People of the United States* (8 vols., New York, 1883–1913), especially in Vols. II, VI, VII, VIII. See also the volumes in D. R. Fox and A. M. Schlesinger, eds., *History of American Life* (12 vols., 1927–) by C. R. Fish, A. C. Cole, A. M. Schlesinger, and P. W. Slosson. The fullest treatment of the subject up to the Civil War is in R. A. Billington, *Protestant Crusade, 1800–1860* (New York, 1938), which lists a large number of special studies, among the more important of which are L. D. Scisco, *Political Nativism in New York State* (New York, 1901), and L. F. Schmeckebier, *History of the Know Nothing Party in Maryland* (in Johns Hopkins University Studies, Series XVII). Material on the A.P.A. movement of the eighteen nineties is noted in Schlesinger's volume, above mentioned (pp. 345–348); see especially H. J. Desmond, *The A.P.A. Movement* (Washington, D. C., 1912). For the

Ku Klux Klan of the nineteen twenties, see P. W. Slosson, *The Great Crusade and After* (History of American Life, XII), 306–314, 451–452, and authorities there cited. Of interest in connection with the election of 1928 are the articles by C. C. Marshall and Governor A. E. Smith in *The Atlantic Monthly* for April and May, 1927.

THE CHURCHES AND SOCIAL LEGISLATION. For the slavery issue, see A. C. Cole, *Irrepressible Conflict* (History of American Life, VII), 255–261, and works cited by him; J. F. Rhodes, *History of the United States since the Compromise of 1850* (9 vols., New York, 1893–1928), II, 50–66, 87–92. There are some pertinent documents and an extensive bibliography in P. G. Mode, *Source Book*, etc., chaps. XXVII and XXVIII. For the attitude of particular churches, see W. W. Sweet, *The Methodist Episcopal Church in the Civil War* (Cincinnati, 1912); L. G. Van der Velde, *The Presbyterian Churches and the Federal Union* (Cambridge, Massachusetts, 1932); and the denominational histories already cited. For general discussions of the function of the church in relation to social action by the state, see W. A. Brown, *Church and State in Contemporary America*, chaps. V–XI and pp. 350–351 (bibliography on the "Social Mission of the Church"); J. A. Ryan and M. F. X. Millar, *The State and the Church*, chaps. IX and X; H. U. Faulkner, *The Quest for Social Justice* (History of American Life), especially chap. IX. Important in this field are the publications of the Federal Council of the Churches of Christ and its various commissions, and those of the National Catholic Welfare Conference. For church policies in relation to marriage and divorce, see the articles on those subjects in *Encyclopaedia of the Social Sciences* (5 vols., New York, 1930–1935) and the *Catholic Encyclopaedia*. The position of the Catholic Church is authoritatively defined in the encyclical of Pius XI, "On Christian Marriage," 1931. For church activities in regard to liquor legislation, see, for earlier phases, J. A. Krout, *Origins of Prohibition* (New

York, 1925), and E. H. Cherrington, *The Evolution of Prohibition in the United States* (Westerville, Ohio, 1920); and for later developments, P. Odegard, *Pressure Politics: the Story of the Anti-Saloon League* (New York, 1928). Two notable declarations of the Papacy on economic issues are the encyclical of Leo XIII, "On the Condition of Labor" *(Rerum Novarum)*, May 15, 1891; and that of Pius XI, "on Reconstructing the Social Order" *(Quadragesimo Anno)*, May 15, 1931. An example of a Protestant statement on this subject is that of the Methodist Episcopal Church, May 1908, in H. S. Commager, *Documents of American History* (New York, 1934), No. 371.

VI. THE AMERICAN TRADITION TESTED

CHURCH AND STATE IN EDUCATION. The following are useful reference works: A. W. Johnson, *Legal Status of Church-State Relationships in the United States with Special Reference to the Public Schools* (Minneapolis, 1934); S. W. Brown, *The Secularization of American Education* (New York, 1912); Carl Zollmann, *American Church Law,* chap. II (especially useful for citation of judicial decisions); I. L. Kandel, ed., *Educational Yearbook of the International Institute of Teachers College: the Relation of the State to Religious Education* (New York, 1933); J. A. Burns, *The Growth and Development of the Catholic School System in the United States* (New York, 1912); R. J. Gabel, *Public Funds for Church and Private Schools* (Washington, D. C., 1937); the article on "Education" in the *Catholic Encyclopaedia.* For the schools' controversy in New York in the middle years of the nineteenth century, see W. O. Bourne, *History of the Public School Society of the City of New York* (New York, 1873); the biographies of Archbishop John Hughes by J. R. G. Hassard (New York, 1866) and H. A. Brann (New York, 1892) and his *Complete Works* (ed., L. Kehoe, 2 vols., New York, 1864); and A. J. Hall, *Religious*

Education in the Public Schools of the State and City of New York (Chicago, 1914). See for references to other special studies: W. A. Brown, *Church and State in Contemporary America*, 352.

Index

Maryland, 53; his toleration policy, 54–55

Calvert, Charles, third Lord Baltimore, on colonization of Maryland, 54

Calvert, George, first Lord Baltimore, and the founding of Maryland, 53–56

Calvin, John, Church-State of Geneva, 9, 15, 17–18; *Institutes of the Christian Religion*, 15, 16, 17; writes to Gaspard de Coligny, 16; on church and state, 16–17

Cambridge Agreement, 20, 38

Cambridge Platform, 39–40

Canada, church-state relations in, 27–28

Carolina, religious liberty in, 59–60; *see also* North Carolina and South Carolina

Carroll, Charles, member of committee conferring with Canadian Catholics, 77

Carroll, Father John, with committee conferring with Canadian Catholics, 77

Cartwright, Thomas, attitude toward church-state relations, 19

Catholic Church, and the Edict of Nantes, 8; legal status of in England, 13–14; legal incorporation of church property, 107; attitude toward church-state relations, 112; and divorce legislation, 115–116; and the law of marriage, 115–116; and economic issues, 116–117; its stand on education, 119–120; its position toward public aid to church schools, 124; objects to instruction by Public School Society, 124; on parochial schools, 126; objection to Bible reading in schools, 128

Catholics, resistance against the established Anglican Church, 13–14; in New France, 26; in Virginia, 34; priests banished, 43; Maryland a col-

ony for, 53; and Protestants in Maryland, 54–56; in Pennsylvania, 58; after English and colonial revolutions, 63–64; gradual change in attitude toward, 77; worship protected by law in Massachusetts, 80; number increased by European immigration, 102; agitation against, 110

Chaplaincies, civilian and military, 82–83

Chaplains in our federal government, 96

Charter of Privileges, 58

Child, Dr. John, 42–43

Child-labor legislation and the Catholic Church, 116

Christian commonwealth idea after Protestant Revolution, 7

Church and state, in Europe, 2–9; in America today, 3; interlocking between, 5–6, 13; in medieval times, 6; coöperation after Protestant Revolution, 6–8; in Colonial America, 10; Calvin's writing on, 16–17; Tudor system contrasted with City-State of Geneva, 17–18; separation of in Virginia, 87–88; separation of in Connecticut, 88; separation of in Massachusetts, 88–93; relation between as stated by Pope Leo XIII, 103–104; coöperation in higher education, 121

Church and state relations, English parish an example of, 15; state control in New Spain, 23–25, 26; Canadian, 27; in New Netherland, 28–31; in Virginia, 31–33, 35; in English colonies, 31–45; in Massachusetts Bay Colony, 37; set forth in Cambridge Platform, 39–40; bearing of proprietary system on, 52–55; in state constitutions, 78–80; legal aspect of, 106–108; attitude of Catholic Church toward, 112; slavery an issue in, 113–114; education in, 119–120

New France, church-state policy, 26–28; *see also* Canada

New Jersey, church-state relations in, 60

New Light preachers curbed, 67–68

New Netherland, variety of religious elements in, 28; Charter of Freedoms and Exemptions, 28–29; Dutch West India Company, 28–29; public worship in, 29–30, 31

New Side Presbyterians, increase in number of, 86

New Spain, church-state relations, 23–25

New York (city), Public School Society, 124, 125; Board of Education created, 125

New York (state), Church of England in, 60–61; religious liberty in, 60–61; Duke's Laws, 61; royal instructions to governor of, 63; policy toward Catholics, 64; constitutional clause on religion, 79–80; qualifying clause on religious liberty, 98; religious education in, 130

New York Post-Boy, 74

North Carolina, bars non-Christians from holding office, 95

Northwest Ordinance, two clauses on religion, 83

Norton, John, urges prosecution of Quakers, 43

Oklahoma, polygamy prohibited in, 99

Old School Presbyterians, Southern members withdraw from, 114

Old Testament story of Naaman, 134–135

Oregon, law against parochial schools declared invalid, 3; constitution prohibits religious tests, 95; statute regarding public-school education, 127

Pacifists, Supreme Court decisions on, 140–144

Papal encyclicals, Leo XIII, 103–104, 112, 135; Pius XI, 112, 115, 119–120, 127–128

Parish, English, an example of church-state relations, 15

Parker, Theophilus, on the Religious Freedom Act, 90

Parochial schools, 123–132; forbidden public money, 125

Passport oath defined by Department of State, 140

Peace and war, Quaker attitude toward, 58, 114–115

Penn, William, his principles, 56–57, 59; *The Great Case of Liberty of Conscience,* 56–57; receives royal grant of Pennsylvania, 57

Pennsylvania, royal grant to William Penn, 57; Declaration of Rights, 79; abolishes religious tests, 95

Philip II of Spain, control over clergy, 8; decree regarding ecclesiastical appointments, 24–25

"Pious Fund" dispute, 23

Plymouth Colony, compared with Massachusetts Bay Colony, 37

Politics, and religion during Revolutionary movement, 70, 73; in religion, 108–109, 110–111; party politics and religion, 109–111

Politiques, 9

Polygamy, abandoned by Mormons, 98–99

Popes, Pius V, 13; Clement X, 27; Leo XIII, 103–104, 112, 135; Pius XI, 112, 115, 119–120, 127–128

Prayer, Book of Common, Parliament controls changes in, 10–11

Presbyterians in Massachusetts, 42; promised toleration in Virginia, 67, 68; in New York, 71; "General Assembly," 85*n*; attitude toward slavery, 113